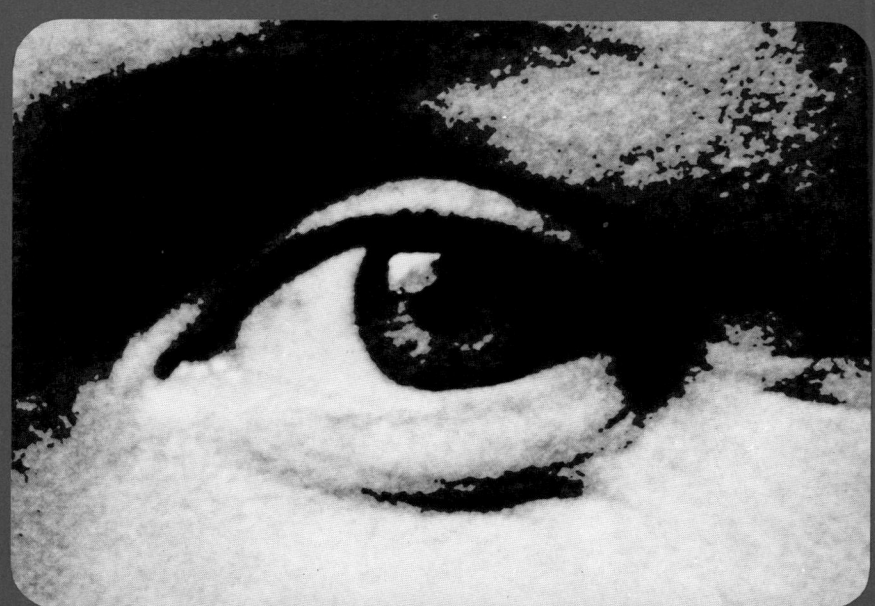

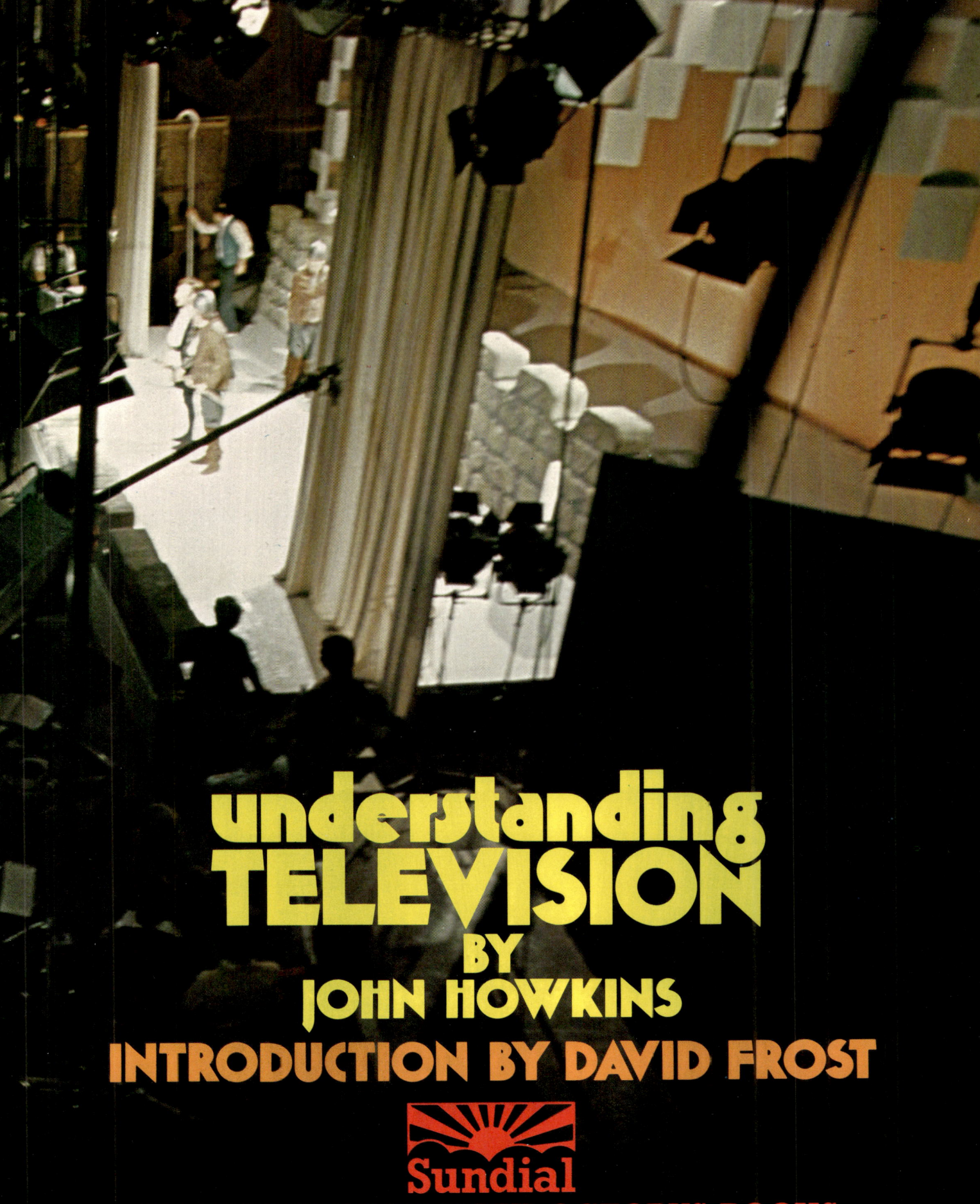

Designed by Tod Slaughter, Arka Graphics

First published 1976 by
Sundial Books Limited
59 Grosvenor Street, London W1

© 1976 Sundial Books Limited

ISBN 0 904230 01 5

Produced by Mandarin Publishers Limited
22a Westlands Road, Quarry Bay, Hong Kong

Printed in Hong Kong

Contents
6 INTRODUCTION
11 THE TELEVISION REVOLUTION
31 INSIDE TV
51 BRINGING BACK THE NEWS
62 PRODUCING DRAMA FOR TELEVISION
76 THE TV SYSTEMS AND PROGRAMMES OF THE WORLD
106 TELEVISION GOES LOCAL
124 GLOSSARY
125 INDEX
128 ACKNOWLEDGMENTS

INTRODUCTION

'Mr. Ruskin, we have laid a cable to India! We can talk to India!'
'And what, pray, do you want to *say* to India?'

Television was once described as an instrument whereby you are entertained in your living room by people you would not have in your house. By the standard of many current comments about the medium, that is almost a compliment. Critiques come thick and fast.

In *The Ravenous Eye*, Milton Shulman takes a bleak view. 'It sits there in the corner of the living-room relentlessly transmitting its mosaic of life. Image after image, incident after incident, emotion after emotion, juxtaposed with anarchic, confused and irresponsible logic. A man, doused in petrol, sets fire to himself outside the White House. A dentist discovers a gas to destroy mankind. Which is true? Which is false? Does it matter?'

In *Who Does She Think She Is?*, Mary Whitehouse reports: 'I had a call from a friend, highly intelligent, very down to earth and with a great sense of humour. For rather sad and personal reasons she had never married and had never seen a naked man. She had watched the programme the previous evening and had suddenly found herself confronted by a male nude in her living room.'

In *The Shadow in The Cave*, Anthony Smith muses: 'For a long time we in Britain thought that the success of our broadcasting lay in the "quality" of the programmes. That was in part true, but in reality the success of the BBC (and ITV, at certain periods) has been that it conscientiously reflects the success of a whole culture in finding some kind of valid relationship with the mass audience, the society at large. That relationship, in Britain as elsewhere, is now under strain and to that extent our "system" is no longer adequate, no matter how great the quality of individual programmes.'

In his celebrated speech as Chairman of the FCC, Newton Minow told the National Association of Broadcasters on May 9th, 1961: 'I have confidence in your health, but not in your product. I invite you to sit down in front of your television set when your station goes on the air . . . and keep your eyes glued to that set till the station signs off. I can assure you that you will observe a vast wasteland.'

Charles Sopkin, who locked himself in his New York flat in April 1967 with five television sets and watched the entire output from 7 am to 3 am every day, went even further: 'Well, what can one say? That the networks are trying? They obviously aren't . . . I naïvely expected that the ratio would run three to one in favour of trash. It turned out to be closer to a hundred to one.

will freely confess that, immediately after my week-long ordeal, thought that the only way to solve TV's problems was, literally murder – to send in squads of machine gunners and summarily execute every executive at every network and start from scratch.

That is clearly overkill, in more sense than one. But television does seem to encourage extreme reactions – both of devotion and of antipathy. Malcolm Muggeridge – who always underrates, I think, the contribution he has made through television – said on one occasion: 'The villain, the enemy, is the camera. We who are accustomed to working with it know that it is capable of infinite deception, probably the greatest of all deceptions, and yet is accepted as having some kind of objective truth in it.'

However well expressed, that comment overestimates the power of television and underestimates the intelligence of the audience. Eamonn Andrews once said: 'I don't believe in the power of television. No one is ever influenced by television who doesn't want to be.' Perhaps the audience reaction is not quite as deliberate as that, but Eamonn has seized on the key word – for television has influence rather than power. And it is not the sort of influence that can create a Damascus experience that is contrary to the conscious will or subconscious inclination of the viewer.

Television may perhaps articulate a feeling not yet articulated, express a thought the viewer had not fully formed – but *Cathy Come Home*, for example, would not have had the catalytic effect it did on the fight against homelessness unless the audience had felt deep down that homelessness was out of place or indeed abhorrent, in a so-called affluent society. *Cathy Come Home* did not convert its audience; it rallied them to a cause in which they inherently believed even if they had never previously expressed it.

But even if the influence of television operates within these pre-ordained perameters, nevertheless it *is* influence and therefore, of course, society's continued vigilance is essential. Every responsible producer welcomes it – and, even if the public reaction is hostile, can always console himself with the thought that it does at least prove that somebody is watching. (Though if, at the end of a tirade, the complainant goes on to say, 'Of course, I did not see the programme *myself* . . .', that is really maddening!)

The television producer is subject to another discipline, another particular form of watchfulness, as well. As Antony Jay has pointed out: 'Every producer's work goes straight into the sitting room of the Governors, the Chief

Executive, the Board and all his superiors and colleagues. And you cannot placate an angry MP by saying he must have been unlucky and received a defective model of *Panorama* which you will happily replace at once and free of charge.'

If the topic is close to the viewer's heart, then, as Jay goes on to observe, a new irregular verb rapidly comes into being: 'I can make things clear to ordinary people; you over-simplify; he trivialises.'

The massive audiences television attracts often bring with them another form of negative feed-back – the resentment of an intellectual elite. I have never understood why the decision of the individual man or woman at the ballot box is regarded as the valid and binding exercise of his democratic function, while the decision he or she might make in the evening at the 22-inch box is so often dismissed as the invalid act of a moron. Popularity is no more or less of an indictment of a programme than electoral victory is of a political leader. For it *is* possible, in the words of the old books of BBC matches, 'To make good programmes popular and popular programmes good.'

The public taste may not be for all the categories that some sociologists or producers might wish. For example, it is clear that the public does not switch on to documentaries in the same numbers as it switches on to comedy shows. Nevertheless, within each category it makes some pretty shrewd judgments after the event – *Laugh In*, *Flip Wilson* and *All in the Family* were the most refreshing comedy programmes when they first topped the US ratings. It was the same in Britain with *Till Death Us Do Part*, *Steptoe* and *Please Sir*.

The other important point, of course, is that these are judgments *after* the event. There is still, thank God, no computer that can foretell the public's reaction *before* the event. Computer researchers may claim so – but in fact they can only operate on previously known reactions to previously known factors. There is still room for the professionals to take the leap of the imagination that may initially terrify the marketing departments. I have myself all too often heard the prophets of doom talking about the hopeless prospects for, say, *TW3* in England or 90-minute interviews in America. The truth of the matter was that since both were strange new animals, there was nothing against which to measure the potential public response. So the pundits turned out to be wrong, and the absurd, unscientific 'hunches' turned out to be right.

Peacetime television has been operating in the West for only 30 years. When one compares what the developments were in film in *its* first 30 years as opposed to later, one realises again how difficult it is to predict the future course of television. Dorothy Todd Henant, a producer with the Canadian Challenge for Change community film project says: 'There is no doubt about it. It's here. Half-inch video is everywhere, and so are cable companies and the number of people behind the cameras and in front of the cameras is multiplying unbelievably. Television will no longer be the medium of a small elite, programming for the masses. It will be the forum through which the many segments of the community will be able to talk to each other, a medium for everybody.'

Writing in the *Saturday Review*, Isaac Asimov said: 'There are no boundaries in the global village . . . world government will become a fact even if no one, due to past prejudices, particularly wants it, and perhaps even if no one is particularly aware that it is taking place.'

George Stoney, Co-Director of Alternative Media Center in New York asked: 'If the public were free to make its own television, what would it be like?'

And Thea Sklover of the Open Channel, New York, sees a world in which. 'Every young person should have the skills of video, just the way they have the skills of writing.'

Cable television may or may not realise its full potential (though I think there is a pretty good prognosis for the station in Sheffield with the notice on its bulletin board, 'Anyone who says: "That is all we have time for", will be fired!'). And like television itself, it is not always clear what its full potential is. I think back to a thought-provoking conversation with one of the foundling fathers of the cable industry who was explaining to me how one day quite soon the viewer will not only have a set that enables him to choose from one of 40 programmes to watch, but even from one of 40 programmes in which to participate. 'Each viewer will have a camera in his room,' the founding father explained. 'Whenever he chooses he will be able to switch the camera on. Of course, in a totalitarian society, the problem will come in switching the camera *off* . . .'

But that is hopefully only a visionary's nightmare. For all the men and women working in television today, the words of Edward R. Murrow still ring true. 'This instrument, television,' he said, 'it can entertain, it can inform, yes, and it can even inspire. But it all depends on the will of the humans who operate it. Otherwise it is just lights and wires in a box.'

That was Edward R. Murrow's challenge to his generation. The challenge is the same today.

David Frost

THE TELEVISION REVOLUTION

The Apollo 11 moon landing turned the world into one global village. When Neil Armstrong stepped out of Apollo 11 on 21 July 1969, at 2.56 GMT, more than 600 million people were ready and waiting to watch him take the 'giant step for mankind'. NASA, the American space agency, got the pictures back to Earth at 11,160,000 mph. They took three seconds. For many people, the awesome sight of Neil Armstrong on the moon, *live*, was 1969's most astonishing and exciting moment.

The TV pictures had another purpose. NASA scientists took a succession of Polaroid snapshots off their TV monitors which, when enlarged, enabled the geophysicists to pick out odd-looking rocks and stones. Within seconds, NASA could tell the astronauts to investigate.

Christopher Columbus is believed to have landed in the New World around September 1492. We don't know the exact date, and he was not sure about the place. His backers in Spain and Portugal did not know whether he had failed or succeeded; and stayed ignorant until he returned over 12 months later. Between Christopher Columbus and Neil Armstrong there was a revolution in communications. The TV link of Apollo 11 had confirmed Marshall McLuhan's 'global village'.

Print, said McLuhan, had broken up society into many small groups. The electronic media (telephones, radio, television and everything else that owes its existence to electricity) have reversed the procedure. The new media are creating one big tribe, an electronic global village. Stockbrokers in New York and farmers in Borneo watch the same Westerns and the same TV ads for the same soap powders. Everybody is involved in everybody else's lives – and problems.

Three years after Apollo 11 had landed on the moon, the global villagers came together again to make the 21st Olympic Games the Earth's biggest and most spectacular. An estimated 450 million people saw Valerie Borzov win the 100 metres and Mark Spitz gain his seventh gold medal (and the estimated audience for the 1976 Olympics is one billion). Those TV highlights were the result of an electronic operation that was unique in its size, complexity and extravagance. A total of 3,700 TV and radio people (1,200 journalists and 2,500 technicians) converged on the Olympic city. In the main stadium, each of them had a personal TV monitor, a direct link to the GOLYM information computer and a radio telephone.

The television signals were produced by a German consortium, DOZ, who transmitted to 110 countries from 9 am to 11 pm every day (the BBC, the American ABC and the Italian RAI used their own private lines). DOZ collected the pictures from the 33 different Olympic stadia, converted them into the appropriate foreign TV technical standards and sent them to one of three special ground stations for transmission to the Atlantic satellite (for the Americas and Africa) or the Indian Ocean satellite (for Asia and Australia).

The DOZ timetable was rigid and precise. Let's see how they covered the first heat of the important 100 metres on 31 August. The track officials called the competitors at 10.30 am (Munich time) and compiled the final list of runners at 10.50. The heat started promptly at 11.00 and finished 10·45 seconds later. Within 35 seconds the photo-finish had been developed and printed and, still within the minute, the winner and his time had been electro-printed on the stadium scoreboard and on worldwide television. Viewers in Los Angeles, for instance, received pictures of the race 54 seconds after 11.00 (just after 2 am, local time). So did viewers everywhere else – Rio de Janeiro, Dakar, Moscow, Sydney and so on.

Spectators and journalists in the stadium itself had to wait rather longer. The competition management took seven minutes to print the first 100 copies of the top-priority results sheets. The viewer in Los Angeles could be back in bed before the Olympic officials had written proof of what he had just seen.

The power of television was personified by the astounding 'instant fame' of Mark Spitz. Within ten days he had become the world's most famous sportsman and able to command a quoted $5,000,000 for turning professional. The other side of TV's coin was more sombre. The television coverage tempted Black September, the Palestinian guerrilla group, to demonstrate violently against the Israeli team. They killed 11 Israelis and wounded others. The world gasped but continued with the Games.

These unique events attract special audiences. But television is a 24-hour activity. The European Broadcasting Union (EBU) demonstrates this very well. The EBU is the world's oldest club of television broadcasters. Its members include all of Europe's 34 broadcasting organizations. Britain, for example, is represented by the BBC, IBA and ITCA; Italy by RAI. (Governments are excluded.) TV organizations in overseas countries including the United States, Japan, Canada and Australia have joined as associate members.

Every day the EBU holds an electronic market for television news. The market opens at 10.45 am. The EBU coordinator welcomes each member as they tune in on the

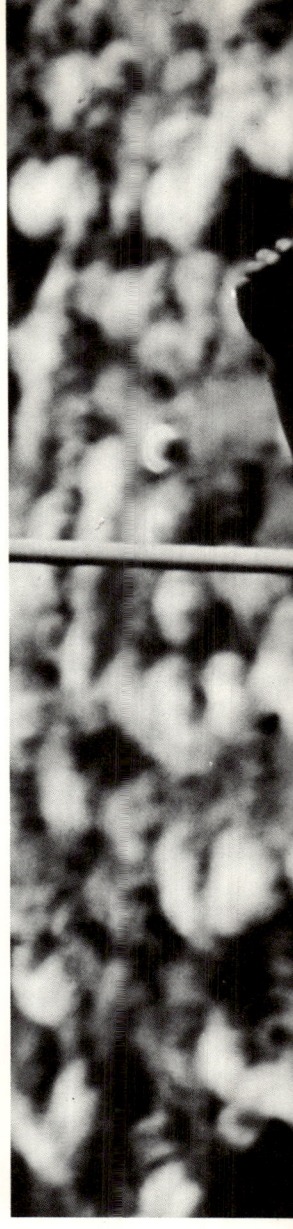

Union's own TV network (Eurovision) and asks them, in turn to describe the stories on offer. The bigger countries like Britain, Germany and France usually have the largest number of stories to sell, often six or seven. After the 'seller' has listed his stories, the coordinator asks, 'Anyone interested?' and members indicate if they want to buy. It is usually the smaller countries, who cannot afford their own film crews, who are most eager. Portugal's television stations (serving only 500,000 sets) and Yugoslavia's JRT (serving only two million) may take several stories every day. After the sellers have announced their offers, countries can ask for specific stories. Vatican City, for instance, may ask for stories about the Catholic Church; football-mad Italy may ask the Netherlands for a film of last night's match between Ajax and Juventus. These direct requests do not always get results. Ask Spain for film of the recent anti-Franco riots, or France for film of last night's student demonstration, or Turkey for a film of their prisons, and they will politely refuse. And EBU will politely change the subject. EBU is a club and members do not annoy each other.

The richer members, of course, can send in their own film crews (Britain's Granada has sent cameramen into

Television covers high jumps and massacres. During the Olympic Games in Munich, it switched between the hooded Arab guerillas who killed nine Israeli athletes, and Sara Simeoni, representing Italy. Sometimes, TV men get caught: Dubos Popelka had to close his Czech station when the Russians invaded.

Turkey disguised as tourists). Other stations can buy film from the commercial news agencies: if the agencies have it.

The market closes around 11.30 and the EBU compiles a 'bought-and-sold' list which it telexes to all members. The actual exchange takes place on the Eurovision network at 5 pm. If a story breaks late, EBU telexes all members and holds another exchange at 8 pm.

EBU is always open and always ready for a sudden news break. On the morning of 21 August 1968, Russian and Warsaw Pact troops invaded Czechoslovakia. The EBU coordinator heard the first news at 6.30 am. She telephoned the EBU headquarters in Geneva and asked Austrian TV to monitor Czech TV at the border town of Bratislava. ORF, the Austrian TV station, started monitoring at 9 am and continued until Czech television was forcibly closed down by the Russian troops. EBU recorded the pictures and transmitted them over Eurovision to the rest of Europe and by satellite to America.

The EBU, the world's first international television organization, is only 24 years old. We tend to forget how young television is. America has been broadcasting regular TV programmes for 33 years, Britain for only 28.

The BBC, destined to start the world's first regular TV transmissions in 1936, was not keen on the new-fangled gadget, but, courteous as ever, it was prepared to experiment. BBC Television started in 1936 and ran regular services for three years; then closed down for seven years because of the Second World War.

America started one year later in 1937, when NBC, the country's largest radio network, set up a mobile television scanner and transmitter in New York. Like their BBC colleagues, American broadcasters were wary of television. They felt threatened, in fact, exactly as some of their successors feel threatened by today's advent of home video-cassette players and mobile lightweight cameras and recorders.

In the early days, both the BBC and NBC broadcast to a tiny but devoted audience. They were not yet called viewers; nobody had invented the term. The first broadcasters juggled with various terms for somebody who watches television programmes and considered 'watcher', 'observer', 'tele-observer', 'picturer', the ambiguous 'receiver' and the futuristic 'vidion'. Eventually they chose 'viewer'.

Growth was slow. In 1950 only 9 per cent of US homes and 7 per cent of UK homes had sets. But by the mid-1960's television had penetrated into 90 per cent of US homes and given America the claim to be the world's first 'television society'. Britain and Canada soon followed and by the end of the decade they were joined by Japan, Australia, Sweden, France and West Germany.

The American and European figures, of course, were exceptional. The world population in 1960 was about 3,400 million. Compared to this figure, the 1960 world total of 100 million TV sets appears unimpressive. In China, Africa and Asia most people had never seen a TV set, let alone regularly watched programmes. In 1960, China had only 50,000 sets. And until 1972 India had only one TV station, in New Delhi, and it could only reach twenty miles outside the city.

But the trend towards more and more TV societies – towards a TV world – is fast and irreversible. China is determined to use television to educate itself and now has about 600,000 sets. India has embarked on a striking satellite programme and plans a national network by 1980.

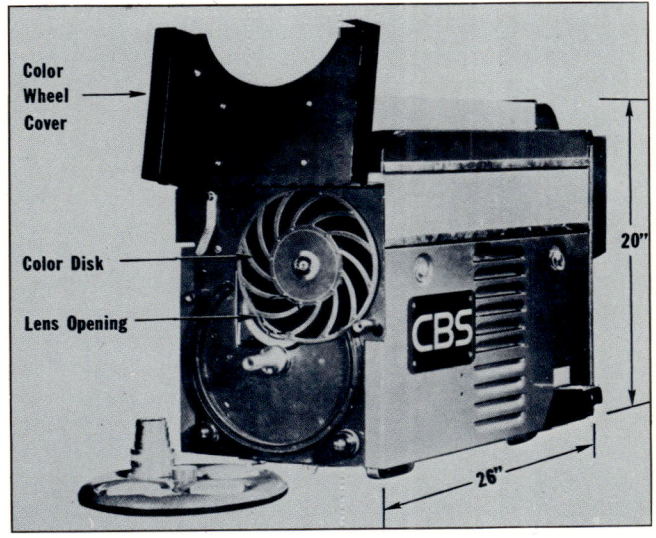

The inventor of the first broadcast television, John Logie Baird, was a quiet, sombre Scotsman. His mechanical system used a series of revolving discs with holes and slits. Early viewers, bottom right, treated the first sets (called Television Receiving Apparatus) as a cross between an altar and a sci-fi monster. Top right, CBS' colour camera, manufactured in 1947, used a colour filter disc.

The first man on the moon, Neil Armstrong, took the photograph, right, of his pilot, Edwin Aldrin. TV audiences were able to see them both together.

The colour camera, left, was used on Apollo 16; it is wrapped in plastic against the cold. In Houston, Gary Scott, below, could control the camera to turn on, off, pan, lift, zoom and adjust to different light intensities.

In 1936, there were 2,000 TV sets. In 1960, around 100 million. Today, there are over 300 million. America's 74 million households own 93 million sets, and the average household watches for 6¼ hours every day. In Britain, the average household watches for 5½ hours; in Australia 4½ hours; in Japan, around 3¼ hours. The world record, according to the respected Nielsen ratings, is the American figures for November 1972: a daily average of 7 hours and 4 minutes.

The basic index for television statistics is the number of households with a TV set (or two or three): the jargon calls them TV homes. America has 74 million homes and 71 million TV homes; a penetration of 96 per cent. Britain has 20 million homes and 19½ million TV homes; a penetration figure of 97 per cent (all 1974 figures).

America and Japan have by far the largest numbers of television stations. America has 933, Japan 102. Australia has 43. Britain has only 16. In 1973 20 per cent of American TV homes could receive at least ten stations; 50 per cent could receive seven. Almost everyone (93 per cent) could receive at least four.

The American audience switches on early and builds to a climax during the evening. In America, 10 per cent of homes are switched on at 7.30 am; by noon, another 30 per cent. In summer, the audience stays at 30 per cent until 5 pm but in winter it gradually rises throughout the after-

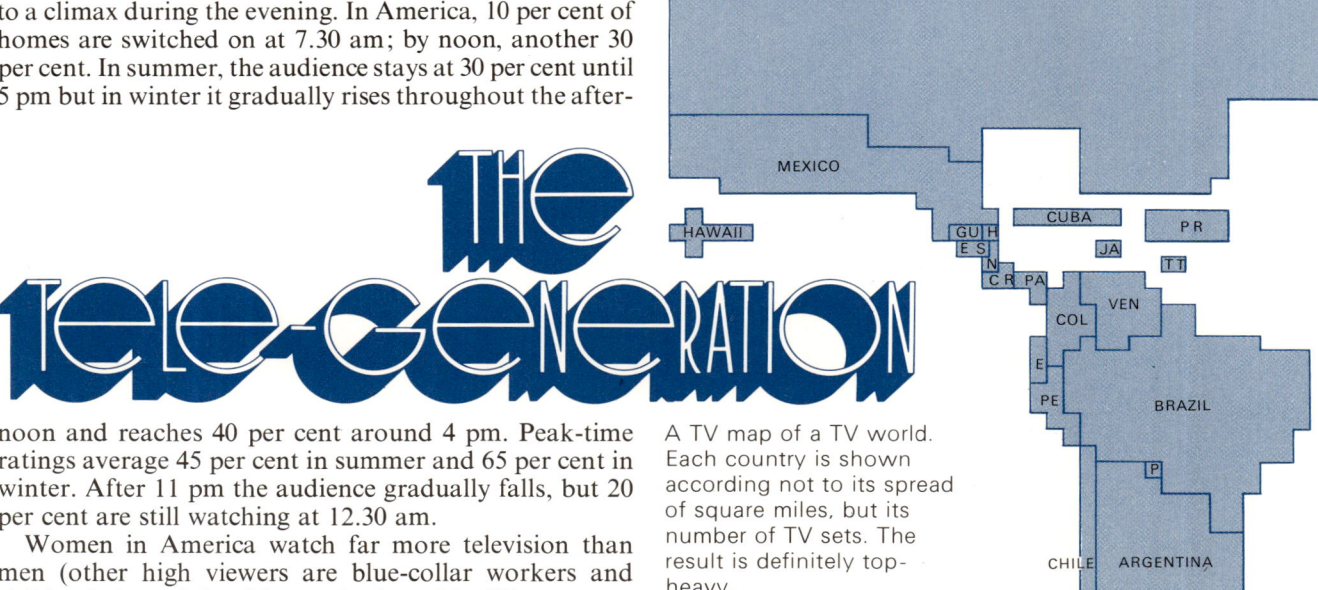

The Tele-Generation

noon and reaches 40 per cent around 4 pm. Peak-time ratings average 45 per cent in summer and 65 per cent in winter. After 11 pm the audience gradually falls, but 20 per cent are still watching at 12.30 am.

Women in America watch far more television than men (other high viewers are blue-collar workers and children). Any night of the week, about 37 million women are watching TV. Men are more changeable and it is their decisions to stay in or go out that raises and lowers the total audience figure. On Sundays they tend to stay in, and Sunday night is the most popular TV night of the week. Programmes are watched by about 60 million people (the exact 1972 statistic is that between 7.30 and 11 pm, an average of 64 million people were watching every minute). Friday night, when men tend to go out, is the least popular, with only 55 million people watching every minute: but 55 million is equal to half the adult population of the U.S. Such is the tele-generation.

Children born into this kind of TV society will spend more time, on average, watching television than working at a job, working at a hobby, eating, attending school or travelling – or anything, in fact, except sleeping.

By the time he is 18 years old, the average American child of the 1970s will have spent 10,800 hours in school but seen 20,000 hours of television.

The children of upper-class 'WASP' Americans spend a comparatively short time – for children – in front of

A TV map of a TV world. Each country is shown according not to its spread of square miles, but its number of TV sets. The result is definitely top-heavy.

the screen. But the children of black and working-class Americans may watch for ten hours or more every day.

Television, after all, is more enjoyable, funnier and reassuring than the school's stark classroom, or even its playground. At home the child can switch channels or turn off. He's the master. At school he has to study and learn. He's a subordinate – and one among many.

The lure of television is obvious and nearly irresistible. Every year more people watch more television. The poor and badly educated are most easily seduced. They often lack the enterprise and initiative, and the hard cash, to generate alternatives that could be more personal and more creative. For these people, it is not religion but television that is the opium of the masses.

By the time he is 75, the average US male will have spent about 9 years of his life watching television. The average Briton will have seen 8 years. These figures assume that viewing figures remain as they are; but, of course, they are much more likely to increase.

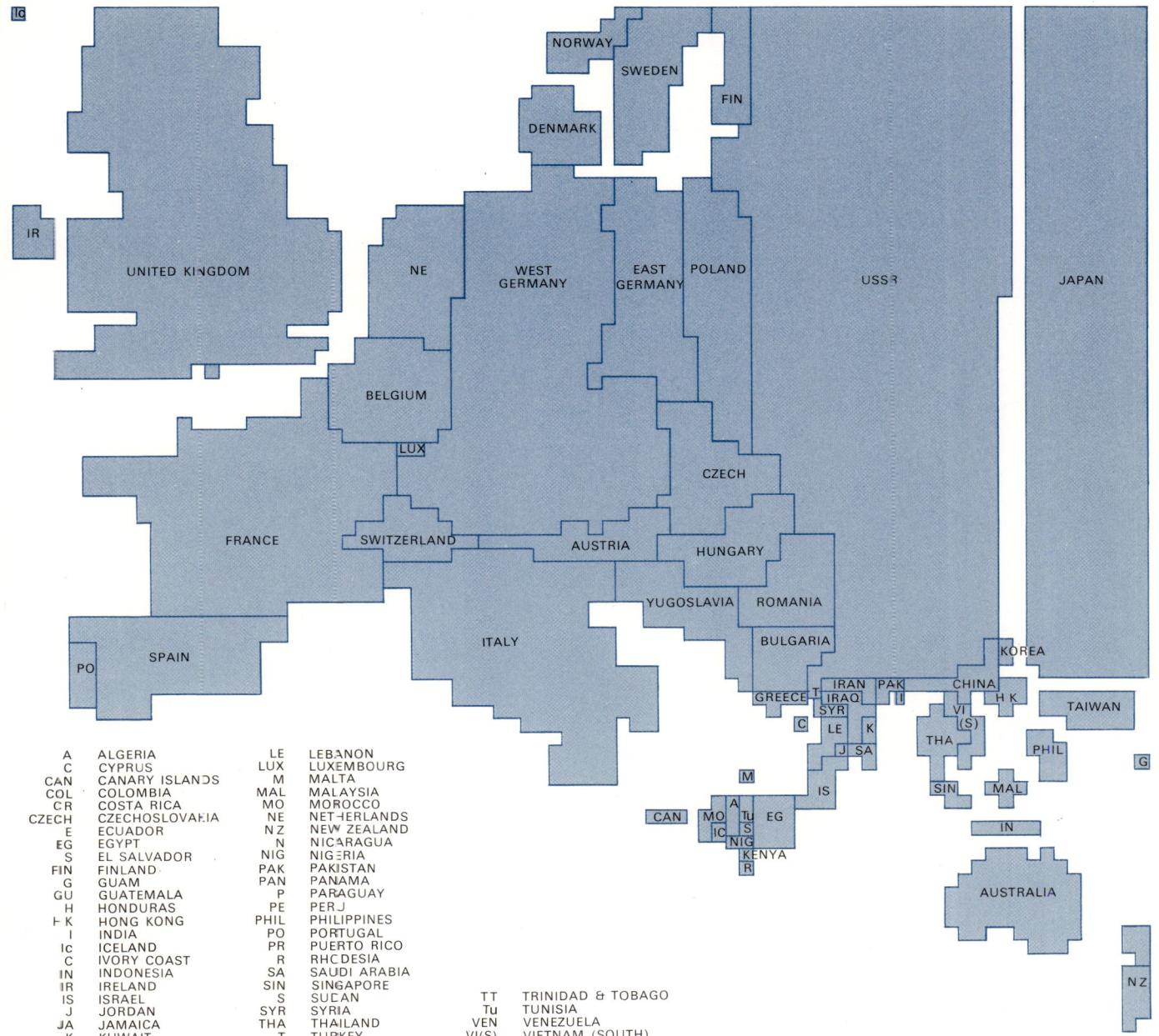

A	ALGERIA	LE	LEBANON			
C	CYPRUS	LUX	LUXEMBOURG			
CAN	CANARY ISLANDS	M	MALTA			
COL	COLOMBIA	MAL	MALAYSIA			
CR	COSTA RICA	MO	MOROCCO			
CZECH	CZECHOSLOVAKIA	NE	NETHERLANDS			
E	ECUADOR	NZ	NEW ZEALAND			
EG	EGYPT	N	NICARAGUA			
S	EL SALVADOR	NIG	NIGERIA			
FIN	FINLAND	PAK	PAKISTAN			
G	GUAM	PAN	PANAMA			
GU	GUATEMALA	P	PARAGUAY			
H	HONDURAS	PE	PERU			
HK	HONG KONG	PHIL	PHILIPPINES			
I	INDIA	PO	PORTUGAL			
Ic	ICELAND	PR	PUERTO RICO			
C	IVORY COAST	R	RHODESIA			
IN	INDONESIA	SA	SAUDI ARABIA			
IR	IRELAND	SIN	SINGAPORE			
IS	ISRAEL	S	SUDAN	TT	TRINIDAD & TOBAGO	
J	JORDAN	SYR	SYRIA	Tu	TUNISIA	
JA	JAMAICA	THA	THAILAND	VEN	VENEZUELA	
K	KUWAIT	T	TURKEY	VI(S)	VIETNAM (SOUTH)	

By the 1970s television had already become the dominant source of news and entertainment in all industrialized countries except South Africa. People turned to television for nightly news, current affairs, sport, movies, comedies, religion, plays, quizzes and documentaries. In 1973 the American National Association of Broadcasters published a survey which showed that 48 per cent of Americans regarded TV as the 'most believable' source of news; 21 per cent chose newspapers, 18 per cent chose radio and 10 per cent chose magazines. This organization of professional broadcasters might have been expected to produce such results. So a similar survey conducted by *The Times* of London is even more impressive. In October 1971 the paper sampled several hundred people listed in the British *Who's Who*. The result was astonishing – and rather frightening. A majority regarded the BBC as more influential than Parliament, the press, the trade unions, the civil service, the monarchy and the Church, in that order. These 'top people' claimed that TV was more powerful than their official elected representatives. They regarded the BBC, a small group of administrators, engineers, journalists and entertainers, as an authoritative and powerful force in society.

Television's intimate inter-relationship with society was dramatically demonstrated by the events of November 1963. On the morning of 22 November, not many Americans knew the whereabouts of their President. But by the evening, everybody knew. President Kennedy was in Dallas. He was shot at 1.30 pm (New York time). The news of the shooting reached the local UPI office a few seconds later and went out on their nationwide news tapes at 1.34. Two minutes later, ABC interrupted their local programmes to announce: 'Three shots were fired at President Kennedy's motorcade in downtown Dallas.' At 1.40 Walter Cronkite cut into CBS's soap opera, *As The World Turns*, to say the same thing, adding, 'The first reports say that the President was seriously wounded.' NBC abandoned *Bachelor Father* a few minutes later.

Television's first coronation and, ten years later, its first murder. Jack Ruby shoots Lee Harvey Oswald in Dallas on November 24, 1963. Half of America saw it live.

The news hit hard: 'I didn't know what to do,' said one housewife in Denver, over 1,000 miles away, 'whether to rush round and tell people or stay close and listen for more.'

UPI, meanwhile, was telling the world. In London, the BBC broke into their television and radio programmes around 6.50 pm (1.50 New York time). Executives at Rediffusion, the London ITV station, heard the news, less formally, from a waitress who, according to one of those present, 'had heard it on the radio and wasn't quite sure if she had got it right.'

Most people heard it on the radio, including Caroline Kennedy and Mrs Oswald. So did Eamonn Andrews, the British broadcaster, who was driving to the SFTA annual Awards Ball to celebrate among others the BBC's senior newsreader, Robert Dougall. Dougall said afterwards, 'I would have given anything to be on duty that night.'

President Kennedy was confirmed dead at 2 pm. The Vice-President, Lyndon Johnson, asked reporters to delay this announcement until he and the President's widow were clear of the hospital. The reporters readily agreed and the news was not released until 2.32. The rest of the world was told within minutes.

Lyndon Johnson took the President's oath aboard the Presidential plane, Air Force One, as it flew back to Washington. At the capital's Andrews Field airport he gave his first television statement as the new President. All three networks carried the speech in full; and followed the new President to the White House and the Kennedy entourage to Bethesda Naval Hospital for the autopsy. Their cameras were still waiting twelve hours later, at 4.30 am, when Kennedy's coffin was taken from Bethesda to the White House.

Americans went to bed late on Friday night – if at all – and got up early. A Chicago University survey records that the average adult spent ten hours watching TV on Saturday and almost as much on Sunday. So most of the nation saw Lee Harvey Oswald being moved to Dallas State Prison and saw Jack Ruby move in front and shoot him point-blank.

It was television's first live murder.

Kennedy was buried on Sunday and people watched that, too, and then on Sunday night they began to realize that life had to get back to normal somehow. But on Monday the networks went back to Washington for the funeral mass and the receptions.

The American networks stayed on the air for three days and nights. They cancelled most of their regular shows and they cancelled all the commercials. In Britain the BBC and ITV did the same for most of Friday night and for the funeral.

During those three days, says the Chicago study, the average American watched television for 31 hours and 38 minutes. Almost every set was turned on. The same study gives a figure of 96 per cent of TV homes against 95 per cent at Senator Robert Kennedy's assassination and 94 per cent for Apollo 11 (and TV started the macabre hobby of measuring deaths by TV ratings).

Americans did not really watch television that weekend for the latest news. The scare of a national plot and hordes of Cuban killers quickly subsided. After the first few hours, news was rare. Instead, they wanted to share in the crisis, to be aware of the pain, to sympathize. Watching television gave them a sense of participation in the American village.

The British had discovered a similar but less widespread sense of participation during the Coronation of George VI (the world's first outside television broadcast) and that of Elizabeth II. The 1953 Coronation of the young Queen made Britain suddenly aware of the fact of being a 'TV society'.

The growing pains of the tele-generation are awkward and confused. As television becomes a mass medium, penetrating into 90 per cent or more homes, it literally *creates* a mass audience.

The process was most obvious and most painful in America where people, communities, and even States

Bangkok, Thailand; Tokyo, Japan; New York, USA: a television world.

had been able to maintain a strong local identity. (America has no truly national newspapers.)

Many Americans did not want to be part of television's mass audience, the mass society, the TV society. They were mostly the older and richer of the nation, but not exclusively. All generations and all income groups combined in one powerful group: the Southern segregationists. They were worried by TV's assumption of society as egalitarian and racially mixed. They attacked several networks' shows that depicted blacks and whites on equal terms. They criticized the *Arthur Godfrey Show* for presenting a black singer. They opposed telecasts of all baseball teams that included black players. In 1956, several Louisiana congressmen even promoted a Bill to ban all television programmes which showed whites and blacks in a 'sympathetic setting'.

In Britain, the powerful conservative National Viewers and Listeners Association (NVALA) has similarly rebuked the BBC for its assumptions about its audience – in other words, about British society. Both groups have tried to reject the broadcasters' vision of society. Both groups want to maintain their own way of life. But both American television and the BBC and ITV, for different reasons, make such conservative independence difficult and probably impossible.

Television has become a central part of life. In America a TV set is a civil right. If you are poor, the Department of Health, Education and Welfare will give you money to rent one. If you go bankrupt, your TV set is excluded from recoverable assets. The German Supreme Court has made a TV set equally sacrosanct in that country.

People's dependence on television was dramatically demonstrated in a 1971 experiment by the Munich Society for Rational Psychology. The Society asked 184 regular viewers to give up television for a year in return for a weekly cash payment. Couples were paid £4, single people £2. Within five months, everyone had gone back to regular viewing.

The affluent, talkative tele-generation is neatly symbolized by the communications satellite. Satellites have changed our concept of distance. They have shrunk the world. A message from London to Paris (227 miles by land and sea) takes the same few fractions of a second and costs the same as one to Buenos Aires (6,951 miles): around the world in 80 deci-seconds, more or less. Let us look more closely at these satellites.

What links Mill Village in Canada and the bridge of Thermopylae in Greece? The answer is an Intelsat satellite. Aristotle, who taught a hundred miles further east of Thermopylae, believed that 'the size of the political unit, the State, was determined by the range of man's voice'. Aristotle obviously favoured small cities and large lungs. Nowadays a man's voice can encircle the world. In 1969 we could even talk to two men on the moon.

A 'ground' station (or 'earth' station), which can transmit and receive signals to and from a satellite and is the key to the Intelsat and every other satellite system, is both an essential telecommunications tool and the latest political status symbol.

When President Nixon visited China in 1972 the Americans and Chinese decided to build a portable ground station at Shanghai so that the American people could see their President mingling with the Chinese, and see this 'live'. The White House enjoyed publicizing the pictures – and the fact that an American corporation had supplied the satellite.

Visiting royalty and heads of State used to plant trees to symbolize their friendship. Nowadays, they prefer to erect a ground station to demonstrate their participation in the telecommunications revolution. The Shah of Persia did this the other way round when preparing for his 1969 visit to the United States. He dedicated a ground station at Asadabad, near Tehran, so that pictures of his meeting with President Johnson could be sent back, live, to Iran.

A satellite transmitting and receiving station in Spain.

Some Heads of State even take a ground station with them. When the Pope attended the International Eucharistic Congress in Bogotá, Columbia, in 1968, his luggage included a portable ground station which was duly erected to beam pictures of His Holiness back to Europe. The Columbians, incidentally, were so impressed with the gadget that they immediately ordered a permanent station for themselves. It opened in the hills to the north of Bogotá in 1970.

Any government can put up a ground station, and most have; any member of the United Nations can join Intelsat, and most have done so. A government has only to buy the station and rent some time with the Intelsat booking agency, Comsat, in Washington or Geneva. RCA supplied the station for China; but most of the major telecommunications corporations are willing to tender. Customers can expect 18 months for delivery and a bill of $2 million.

The first hint of artificial satellites is usually attributed to that wily and provocative visionary Arthur C Clarke. In *Wireless World*, October 1945, he envisaged three satellites 22,300 miles above the Equator: 'At this particular height, a satellite takes exactly 24 hours to complete one orbit and thus stays fixed for ever over the same spot on the Earth. The laws of celestial mechanics can thus provide us with the equivalent of invisible TV towers 22,300 miles high.'

In 1945 neither Clarke nor anyone else expected his prophecy to come true in this century. The first international broadcast, in 1950, was not a success. The BBC are inordinately proud of it, but nobody else was impressed. The French were distinctly not. The BBC, preferring to be British rather than communicative, had broadcast British programmes with British voices. The French were technically unable to receive them; and if they had, they would have had difficulty understanding them.

But Clarke's prophecy did come true. Today there are about twenty satellites in the so-called synchronous orbit 22,300 miles above three spots in the Atlantic, Pacific and Indian Oceans.

The first satellite, of course, was Sputnik, launched on 4 October 1957. To a layman, Sputnik was ridiculously small: a 180-lb ball measuring 23 inches across. But it worked. Everyone outside Russia and, to be sure, everyone inside, too, greeted the news of the glistening, spinning ball with a mixture of shock, delight and awe. The Americans, of course, were also envious. The Defense Department (NASA was not formed until the next year) immediately worked without pause to get an American satellite into the sky. The Russians, meanwhile, had launched Sputnik II – with a dog on board. On 6 December, as Sputnik completed its 1,000th orbit, the US Navy prepared to launch America's first satellite. Alas, it short-circuited on the launching pad and blew up.

Sputnik sped on. In mid-January 1958, it completed its 1,367th orbit and, weary of travelling some 40 million miles, disintegrated (but even that was intended). On 31 January, with a cocky leer at the miserable Navy, the US Army successfully launched the first American space satellite. By the end of 1958 both Russia and America had launched three satellites. Russia had started to bombard the sun (with the successful Lunik) and the

Americans had aimed at the moon (with the unsuccessful Pioneer).

The first satellite to be fitted with a radio transmitter was the American Score. It orbited the Earth transmitting a tape recording of President Eisenhower's 1958 Christmas message. The first satellite to be able to receive *and* transmit was Courier. Launched in 1960, Courier circled the world, receiving messages from America as it passed over Maine, recording them on tape, and transmitting them to Europe as it passed over Devon in southwest England.

The next breakthrough was a satellite that provided TV and telephone circuits. In 1962 Telstar, the first, provided a 22-minute TV link or telephone call before disappearing over the horizon. Intelsat, the first geostationary system, followed within a few years (see page 28).

Since those early days the Earth has launched nearly 4,000 satellites. Every month the Earth's two rocket pads, Cape Canaveral in America and Plesetsk in Russia, add to the total. The *Telecommunication Journal*, the monthly bulletin of the important International Telecommunication Union (ITU), publishes a semi-official list of the month's launches. December 1972, a typical month, included five USSR Cosmos satellites numbered 538–542 for 'scientific measurement'; the USSR's fourth Molnya-II for 'radio communication' (ie, TV and telephones); Germany's tiny Aeros, a yard across, to 'study the atmosphere'; America's BMEWS 1–6, part of its Ballistic Early Warning System with an 'experimental payload'; and America's Samos-91 for 'reconnaissance and surveillance'. The list gloomily admits that Cosmos 538 'decayed on December 27'.

Only a few of the current stock of 4,000 satellites are equipped for telecommunications; and only a fraction of these telecommunication satellites are used for television. The major satellite users are the telephone companies, with their massive traffic in telephone calls and data transmission. In that same month, December 1972, Intelsat's Atlantic satellite provided 2,224 full-time telephone circuits and only 278 hours of television.

But those 278 hours of television are one of the system's more spectacular and potent benefits.

The original satellites, nevertheless, encouraged some disappointing programmes. TV programmes made to celebrate satellite technology have rarely been illuminating of anything except the makers' dogged hopes of an international brotherhood of like-minded television viewers.

The programmes stayed at a low level, but the satellites' technical quality continually improved (a sad imbalance which runs through the entire satellite story). Satellites quickly became more capacious. Early Bird could transmit, at one time, either 240 telephone calls *or* one TV signal. Intelsat IV, the current model, can transmit 6,000 telephone calls *and* 12 TV signals. Intelsat (the organization) bought eight for $108 million and NASA launched four above the Atlantic and two each above the Pacific and Indian Oceans. Intelsat V is expected to be able to cope with 20,000 telephone calls and 20 TV signals.

Future satellites will be larger and – more important – multi-directional. Early Bird could link only two points. In 1965 that was little hardship since only America,

Above: A Syncom satellite (the dark thing on top) is put on the nose of a Delta rocket, ready for launching.

Britain and France had ground stations. But by 1966 Germany, Italy and Canada had opened their own stations and several others were planned. Intelsat satisfied this increased demand by building a 'distribution satellite' that could link more than one station during both reception and transmission. The next stage is the 'broadcast' or 'domestic' satellite which can transmit direct to a domestic receiver on the wall of a house. As Sputnik marked the birth of satellites, the 'broadcast' satellite marks their coming of age.

The domestic satellites, more sharply than their predecessors, raise the question of what satellites are for. Satellites can be used – or misused – in a variety of ways. India and Brazil are keen to beam educational programmes to remote villages.

Other countries are less altruistic. Portugal's colony of Mozambique, with an illiteracy rate of 98 per cent and an appalling education system, receives from its mother country only Spanish soap-operas, *novelas* and American Westerns. Perhaps the Mozambiquans prefer it. Certainly, Venezuela and Puerto Rico are voracious watchers of US baseball.

Let us look at four different ways of using satellites: the international Intelsat system, the Russian Orbita, the Canadian Anik and the Indian SITE.

Right: telecommunications satellites orbiting above the Earth, with their respective ground stations shown in the same colour.

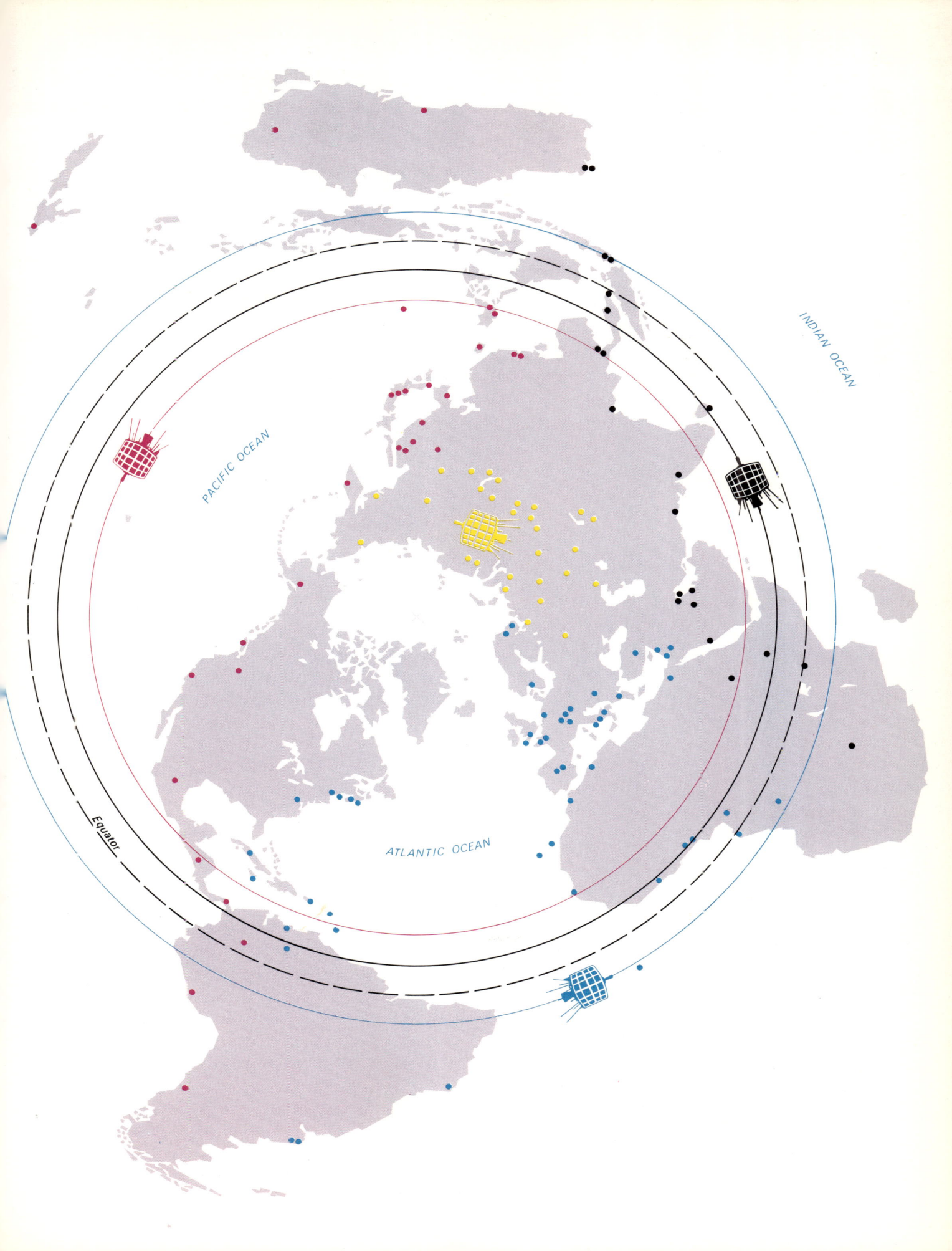

Intelsat is the world's basic international satellite system. The word can mean three things: the controlling body, the network (of nine satellites) and the satellites.

The crucial question in the early 1960s, when the Americans were planning the Intelsat system, was, who should own the satellites. Who should have the right to shoot satellites into orbit and charge rent for their use? The American communications corporations, which had built Explorer, Telstar and the rest, argued that they should. But President John Kennedy had doubts. His belief in public service and public ownership encouraged him to seek a compromise. In the spring of 1962 he submitted to Congress a Bill for a corporation which was half-public and half-private. The debate was fierce. Liberal Congressmen and many foreign countries (notably Russia and Israel) were horrified at the proposal that private American corporations should get even a half-share of such a unique natural resource as space – let alone the valuable synchronous belt, 22,300 miles up, which can only accommodate a limited number of satellites.

The White House, however, was undeterred. It guillotined the debate (a device that no one had used since 1927) and set up Comsat, a mostly private corporation, to grab squatters' rights in the sky. Comsat immediately asked other countries to join in setting up an International Telecommunications Satellite system: Intelsat.

Comsat's first executives fondly imagined that other countries would be glad to join. But they were not. Comsat was greedy – and naive. Greedy, because it retained 61 per cent of the shares in Intelsat, which rather reduced that organization's claim to be an international body (Britain, the next largest shareholder, had only 8·4 per cent), and naive because it assumed it could get away with it. Comsat's brash arrogance led directly to ten years of haggling and frustration.

The sorry result is that the only organization capable of establishing a truly international satellite system has failed to do it. Most inhibiting is the dominant role played by Comsat, which has held on to 61 per cent of the shares and 100 per cent of the management. Secondly, Comsat purposely restricted membership to ITU members, which excluded the People's Republic of China, East Germany and North Korea. Thirdly, Comsat's involvement with AT&T has led to a permanent bias towards telephones and telex transmission at the expense of television.

Intelsat's own members have been openly dissatisfied. In 1975, France and Germany launched their own satellite, Symphonie, orbiting alongside Intelsat's, to link France with French-speaking countries in Africa, Canada and the Caribbean and Germany with its overseas markets. The Russians even publicized a direct rival to Intelsat: Intersputnik.

Intelsat's technical progress has been rapid and mostly first class. Its political and programming work has been elitist and pernickety. Intelsat's real benefits must lie in the future when – and if – its bureaucrats show the same international spirit of cooperation as its engineers.

Russia, Canada, India and Brazil – each is a huge country with immense problems of communication and education. Russia has special problems which explain its reluctance to get heavily involved in Intelsat, or to start its own Intersputnik. She is the wrong size, and in the wrong place, to benefit from a synchronous satellite. She needs a satellite travelling in an elliptical path and crossing Russia in a low diagonal. In 1965 Moscow started its Orbita satellite system which does exactly that. The Molnya satellites swing high over Russia (in order to spread their transmissions over a wide area) and low over America on the other side of the globe. Another Molnya satellite is launched every few months. They provide a succession of reflectors, like a string of pearls, sending telephone calls, television and radio throughout the continent.

The Molyna satellites are in constant use. Russia, in fact, probably sends more television by satellite than any other country. In 1972 her two transmitting stations, in Moscow and Vladivostok, transmitted about 12 hours of television every weekday; an annual total of 3,020 hours. One regular service may soon be copied by other countries. Every morning, Russian TV scans the Moscow newspapers and transmits the main stories throughout Asia.

Canada, like Russia, is another sprawling country. The bulk of its 24 million people live in a narrow strip along the Canadian-US border; but Canada stretches 4,000 miles far to the north of this strip into the Arctic tundra.

The Canadian national Government has wanted a domestic satellite system for a very long time and in November 1972 NASA and Telesat (the Canadian derivative of Comsat) launched the first Canadian satellite, Anik-1. Telesat has tailored Anik's three channels to Canada's two major problems: two national languages and six different time zones. When it is 2 pm in the English-speaking Yukon it's 7.30 in French-speaking Quebec. As one CBC executive said when Anik-1 was launched: 'It's always peak time *somewhere*.'

Anik's Channel One carries the English-language programmes and additional local programmes for the far North, timed for Quebec's peak time; Channel Two carries the same but on a special delay for the North West. Channel Three carries the national French-language programmes and local Arctic programmes timed for Quebec.

Somehow, this system works – except for the Eskimos and Canadian Indians in the Northern Territories. These 250,000 people, living in a vast region the size of Europe, are bitterly disappointed that Anik serves, they say, only 'the transient white people'. For years, the Northerners have been Canada's poor cousins. Their life expectancy was 34 years (in 1969) while the death rate was eight times the national average. Many Northern towns have no telephone (an especially vital link in such a harsh climate) and no radio or TV service. They have complained bitterly that Anik, a once-in-a-lifetime opportunity, has been wasted. Only 55,000 Northerners can receive Anik's programme and most of these programmes, they say, are unsuitable. Telesat have admitted their mistake and promised the Northern communities a greater share in future systems. The next step, in fact, is well suited to isolated remote towns. Telesat and NASA have co-sponsored a sophisticated Communications Technology Satellite (CTS) which beams programmes direct to small, 8-foot, domestic receivers. NASA launched CTS in 1975.

India has different problems. For the first 15 years of independence, until 1962, All India Radio (AIR) had only the one television station in New Delhi with limited range. Mrs Gandhi, minister in charge of AIR and then (in 1966) Prime Minister, was the first senior Government minister to appreciate the need for a national television network. She decided in the late 1960s to use satellites as a short cut to both a national network and – more important – a massive educational programme. India has an illiteracy rate of 72 per cent – that is, about 410 million Indians who cannot read or write.

In 1969 India, the United States and the United Nations signed a remarkably ambitious project for a Satellite Instructional Television Experiment (SITE) whose ATS-6 satellite would beam instructional programmes, mainly on agriculture, to several hundred villages for about four hours every day for a year. The Government commissioned dozens of companies to make special sets and antennae and converters, and rushed them to the chosen villages. People talked of 'alternative technologies' (the antennae were made of chicken wire) and educationists began to prepare year-long research studies.

The ambition was awesome. India proudly imagined groups of villagers clustering round their communal sets in the early evening, when work was done, learning the latest agricultural methods, and understanding them, and rushing out the next day and doing it right. Then the Government got cold feet. Satellites and chicken wire – it sounded slightly ridiculous. NASA, too, was having technical difficulties with its satellite. And educationists began to doubt whether the programmes would actually educate anyone. India postponed SITE to 1974 and then again to 1975.

The Future

The word 'satellite' covers a wide range of objects. The current stock ranges from the sophisticated ATS-6 to the simple Oscar-6. The latter deserves a special mention. An 18-kg spacecraft, it was entirely financed, designed, built and controlled, and is now used, by amateur radio hams. They have built ground stations in the United States, Canada, Australia, New Zealand and Germany and transmitted TV, radio and morse. The current Oscar is the sixth; each one lasts for a year. NASA kindly gave Oscar-6 a piggyback on a meteorological satellite to put it into orbit.

Every year somebody discovers a new use for telecommunications satellites. America's Western Electric wants to distribute movies to cinemas by satellite. It is cheaper, they say, than the current parcel post. The Vatican wants to distribute Catholic programmes to South America. West Germany wants to use a domestic satellite to provide a third television network and Iran wants to have a national educational network. Again, it is cheaper by satellite.

In 1945 people believed that Arthur C Clarke's plans for a synchronous satellite would be stillborn because of the *technical* problems. No one doubted the desirability of global television, or that mankind could produce global programmes that were, at least, watchable. In fact, the opposite has happened. The technical barriers are falling. But nobody is quite sure about the programmes.

Television can be made – and is made, every day – in a variety of places. Streets, racecourses, conferences, mountains, river beds, battlefields and even the moon have served in the past and will serve again. But these places are a technician's nightmare and he will be happier, and his pictures may be better, if he is at home in a studio.

But first, what is TV and how does it work? When most people refer to television they usually mean the programmes or the set. But the word television actually means 'the electronic reproduction, at a distance, of an image'. Television is the making of an image, not the image itself, or the programmes, or the piece of electronic gadgetry that reproduces them. So making television means making an electronic image.

Television, the reproduction of images at a distance, has three main aspects: production, transmission and reception.

A TV producer has to turn his subject – a football match, an old movie, a weekly comedy serial – into an electronic TV signal. He uses three modes: live TV, film, and tape. Live TV is purely electronic and can be transmitted direct. Both film and tape, however, must be converted into an electronic signal in order to be transmitted. The choice of mode (live, film or tape) depends on circumstances. The football match would be transmitted live or recorded on tape for showing later. A big-budget series like *Columbo* would be recorded on film. A cheaper series with mostly interior scenes, like *Till Death Us Do Part* and *All in the Family*, would be recorded on tape.

The essence of a TV camera is its electronic nature. It can produce, instantaneously, an infinite number of identical images. A film camera, on the other hand, produces nothing until its light-sensitive film has been developed (which takes several hours) and further painstaking laboratory work is needed to produce further prints.

After production comes transmission. The newly made TV signal is amplified and transformed into a radio signal and transmitted: either broadcast through the air or cablecast along a cable. The signal is then picked up by a TV antenna (or aerial) and fed to the TV set. Cable signals are delivered, by cable, direct to the set. Finally, both types of signals are reconverted into an image on the set's screen.

This chain of camera-transmitter-receiver only works if each link is plugged into the same kind of AC current, such as a national grid. The local voltage, in fact, is part of each system's television standards, together with the line standard (405, 525, 625 or 815 lines) and the colour standard (NTSC, Pal or Secam). Each country has its own standard.

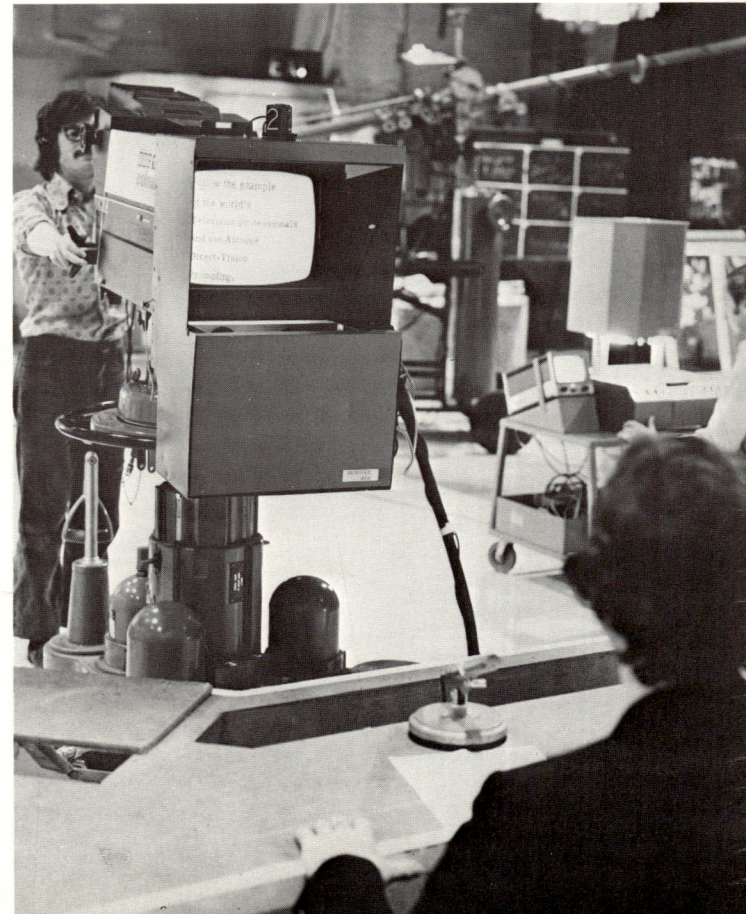

The Pye mark VI camera, top, is used at outside broadcasts to televise sport, etc. When the camera is fitted with a Teleprompter or Autocue, right, the presenter can read his script while looking at the screen. Most national broadcasting studios use the EMI 2001 colour camera

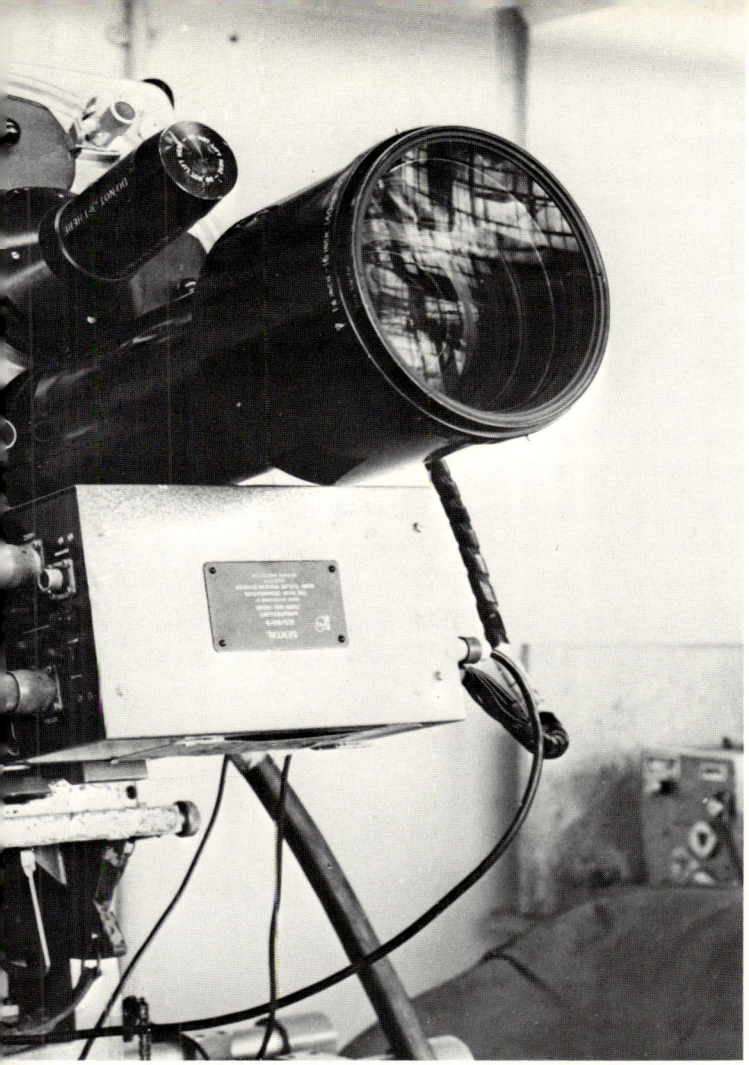

Production: the TV camera

The basic theory of television is very simple. It can be easily understood by thinking of the human eye. The human ear blends sounds together (and notes coalesce into a chord). The eye, however, keeps visual details carefully separate (and objects in a scene remain separate objects). Television, similarly, keeps each visual detail carefully separate in its own space. Otherwise, the eye would see only a blur.

The television camera is designed, therefore, to scan a visual scene and keep every detail precise and separate. TV cameras plugged into a 60-cycle AC current (as in North America) scan such a complete scene every 1/60th of a second. The camera scans from top to bottom from left to right, in a series of horizontal lines. Every complete scan picks up about 175,000 details (the details are usually called 'picture elements').

The heart of a TV camera is a small photo-conductive target that converts these picture elements into voltages (photo-conductive means light sensitive; the camera transforms light energy into electrical energy). It is this continuously varying voltage that constitutes the TV signal.

The critical target is a flat piece of photo-conductive material such as selenium or lead dioxide. Targets vary in diameter from $4\frac{1}{2}$ inches across (in the older image-orthicon cameras) to 1 or 2 inches across (in the newer lightweight vidicon cameras). The camera lens projects the scene on to the front of the target. Simultaneously, a beam of electrons scans the target from the back. The beam creates a small voltage charge in proportion to the brightness of each picture element. When it strikes a bright picture element it induces a high voltage (peak white induces 1 volt). Similarly, a dark picture element induces a low voltage (total black induces 0·3 volts). The picture content of a TV signal, then, consists of a voltage varying from 1 to 0·3 volts.

A TV camera plugged into a 60-cycle AC current in America will generate 60 scans a second. The same camera, slightly adjusted, and plugged into British or

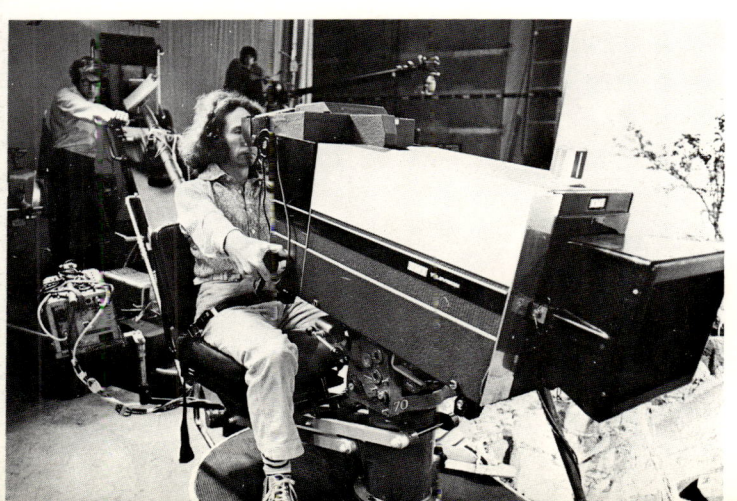

The camera-card for a TV play (here, the episode of *Upstairs Downstairs* described on pages 72–75) lists each camera's shots. The card says move to the spot marked K for a close-up (CU) of Ruby; gently move back to include Rose . . . (another camera takes shot 151) . . . take a three-shot, as before, of Ruby, Rose and Gregory . . . .

Australian 50-cycle AC current, will generate 50 scans a second. The actual scans work in pairs. In the first sixtieth of a second (in the American example) the camera scans alternate lines: numbers 1, 3, 5, 7, 9, 11 and so on until it reaches line 525 at the bottom. Then it quickly does some time checks and returns to the top. In the second sixtieth of a second it scans the remainder: numbers 2, 4, 6, 8, 10 . . . 524.

One scan, completed every sixtieth of a second, is called a field. Every thirtieth of a second, two fields interlace to produce a picture. The whole process, of course, happens so fast that no one ever sees a picture (let alone a field) in the same way as you can see a frame of a filmstrip or the page of a book. Television pictures are electronic messages; they do not exist as objects; they are pure energy.

In Britain and Australia the scanning principle is the same, but the figures are different. The 50-cycle AC current produces a field every fiftieth of a second and a picture every twenty-fifth.

The sheer number of picture elements is staggering: around 7,500,000 (60 × 175,000) every second. Consequently, the entire TV chain (camera-transmitter-receiver) needs a series of complicated and delicate timing devices to ensure that every element knows its right place – and at the right time. An AC current, fortunately, can provide exactly that. Every sixtieth of a second (when the AC current changes or 'alternates' direction), a 'sync' pulse of zero volts 'instructs' the beam in the camera and the matching beam in the receiving TV sets to fly back to the top left-hand corner to start the next field. And at the end of every line, a shorter sync pulse of zero volts instructs both beams to fly back to the left-hand side of the camera and set screen. If you listen carefully, you may be able to hear the sync pulse tone in your own TV set. An American TV camera and set scan 15,750 lines a second (625 × 30) and so emit a tone of 15,750 Hz.

A TV signal, then, is an electrical charge varying from 0·0 to 1·0 volts. The higher voltages, from 0·3 to 1·0 volts, carry the picture information. The regular bursts of zero volts keep the picture in step.

TV production is the act of turning a real-life scene, a film or a tape into a series of voltage charges. Live television transmissions, obviously, present few problems. Tape is also simple. But film is much more awkward. Film is always recorded and projected at 24 frames per second. But TV scans at the rate of 25 or 30 complete pictures per second. In countries like Britain and Australia with a 50-cycle AC current, a TV station can televise a 24-frames-per-second movie at 25 frames per second without noticeable loss (except to movie buffs who, unaware that the film is running one frame fast every second, or four minutes fast every hour, might suspect non-existent cuts).

But American TV stations, working on a 60-cycle AC current, have a major problem. Film shot at 24 frames per second and televised at 30 frames per second appears to be drastically speeded up (the increase is 25 per cent). American engineers have had to develop several ingenious devices to overcome the problem. The most popular called tele-cine, makes the TV camera sample the film in a rhythmic sequence of 30 frames per second. In effect, the camera samples some frames twice.

A TV director can use several special effects to alter the final TV signal. He can borrow, first of all, the production techniques of the movies and re-stage the Battle of Trafalgar in a 3-foot tank. But television's special electronic nature allows him to go much further – he can alter the picture itself. The basic tools of his trade are cuts and mixes; other gadgets include chroma-key or colour separation overlay.

Tricks of the trade

These instant 'Action Replays' of soccer goals, cricket lbw's and baseball runs are recorded, while they happen, on a gold disc which is simply replayed to provide the TV replay. The disc can take 30 seconds of action; played back, it can provide minutes of slow motion. It's a simple but expensive toy.

The teleprompter

The early days of television were adventurous and hectic. Many experienced actors, when confronted with a strange-looking TV camera, completely forgot their lines. They (and their audiences!) were relieved when the invention of videotape enabled them to record their performances. But newsreaders and others who performed live could not use videotape. They had to wait for a different invention: the teleprompter or, in its British version, the autocue.

A teleprompter allows the performer to look the viewer straight in the eye while simultaneously reading his script. Most TV performers can use a teleprompter without showing it (and the public might be surprised at the number of well-known people who use a teleprompter when appearing to speak spontaneously). Users can sometimes be detected by their glazed expression, with the occasional sideways flicker of the eyes, and by their need always to speak at the same pace.

The heart of a teleprompter is a glass reflector fixed slightly below and in front of the camera lens. The script is typed out in large letters, usually five or six words to a line, and wound on to a drum. As the performer starts to speak, the drum is unwound and the script is reflected on to the glass sheet in front of the lens.

The early teleprompters were enormous, complicated and unreliable. The modern ones are neat and simple, and usually reliable. But sometimes the roller goes too slow or, worse, too fast and the performer, with an increasingly agonized look on his face, has to search his memory as the words flash by.

President Johnson had very bad luck during one TV broadcast about Vietnam. He had had installed in his private TV studio a teleprompter which was specially focused for his contact lenses. He was in a hurry that day and strode into the studio and started talking, live, without making any preparations. When he looked at the camera to check his script he could see, reflected in the teleprompter's glass, only the magnificent but irrelevant Presidential seal. He flinched but went on speaking, from memory, to the end. Afterwards, he discovered that the cameraman had refocused the glass for normal eyesight. The President was not amused.

Cuts and mixes

The television image, as we have seen, is actually composed of about 175,000 squares or dots. TV engineers quickly discovered that they could manipulate these squares in different ways. They could switch from one set of squares to another set in a split second, and they could mix squares from one picture with squares from another.

A TV director can cut by the simple method of pressing a 'cut' button on his control console which instantaneously cuts off camera #1 and cuts in camera #2. To mix, he has to move two mixing slides, or mixers. He can move, say, camera #1's video signal from full to zero while at the same time moving #2's from zero to full. Camera #1's picture would be replaced, gradually, by camera #2's. Halfway through the mix, the viewer would have seen both cameras' pictures superimposed on each other. At the end of the mix, he would see a completely new picture. A mix, in effect, is like a slow cut: the viewer sees it happen. Directors often use cuts to convey fast action and excitement, whereas they use mixes to convey a smoother, more restful or sometimes more ambiguous mood.

Some TV directors specialize in mixes. The director

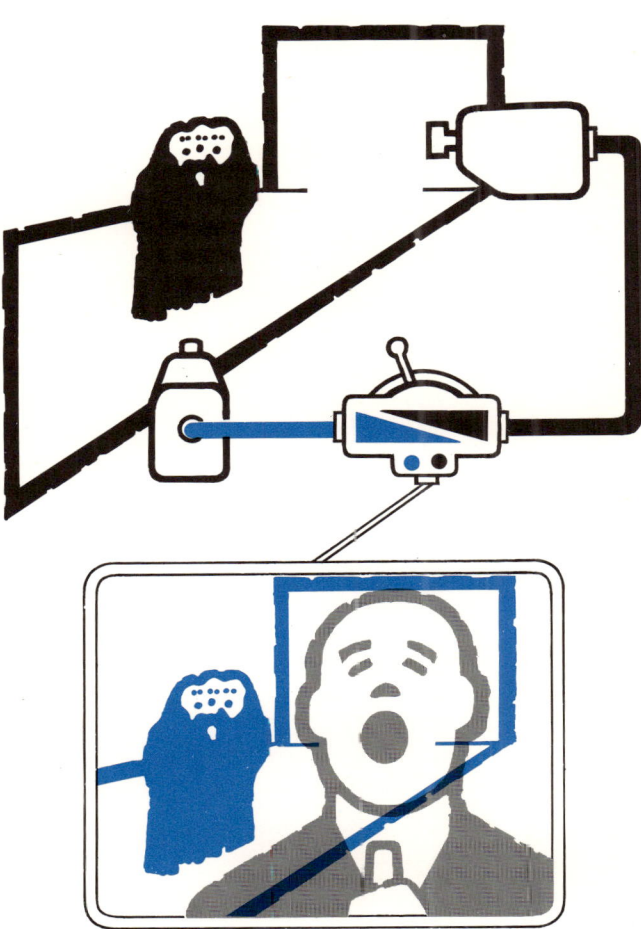

of a variety show, for instance, might have four or five cameras with an almost infinite capacity for complicated mixes. He could position camera #1 to give a long shot of the entire stage, and camera #2 to show the band and the remaining three to cover the compère and his guests. The director could start with using camera #2 for an establishing shot; then fade in camera #4 showing the compère. If camera #4 showed the compère on the right of the screen, the director might ask camera #1 to produce a full-length shot of him on the far left. The director could then fade out cameras #1 and #2 and leave camera #4; or cut to camera #5. This kind of continual mixing may look fussy and self-conscious. But a good director can make it a success.

German TV is world-famous for electronic trickery.

Chroma-key

Chroma-key is even more impressive than mixing, since it appears to mix pictures from two completely different sources. News film can be made to appear on an apparently blank wall behind the newsreader. In drama, the actors can appear to be acting 'in' a painting or cartoon.

The trick is actually simple. It depends on the chrominance (or colour) of one picture keying (or triggering) the signal of another. A colour camera #1 focuses on the performer (newsreader, actor) and produces a TV signal. The chroma-key matrix, the black box of the operation, scans camera #1's image and, whenever it sees the chosen colour (usually blue), it substitutes camera #2's signal.

Imagine camera #1 shows a little girl against a blue backcloth, and camera #2 shows a table leg. The chroma-key matrix scans the girl and the backcloth and whenever it sees the blue backcloth it substitutes the image coming from camera #2. So the little girl appears to be looking at a huge table leg – Alice in Wonderland.

Blue or yellow are usually chosen because they are the opposite of flesh tones. The colours, of course, must be strictly controlled. If Alice had been wearing a blue necklace, bits of camera #2's picture would have appeared in a ring around her neck.

Transmission and reception

The final TV signal will be sent to a transmitter and transmitted as an AM radio signal (the audio signal is sent FM). The two signals will travel through the air or along a cable to domestic TV sets where they will reappear after going through the same process as in the original TV camera – but in reverse. A gun in the set's cathode tube (similar to the gun in the camera tube) beams electrons at the inside of the TV screen. The electrons cause the 175,000 phosphor dots to glow, and produce a line-by-line image of the original scene.

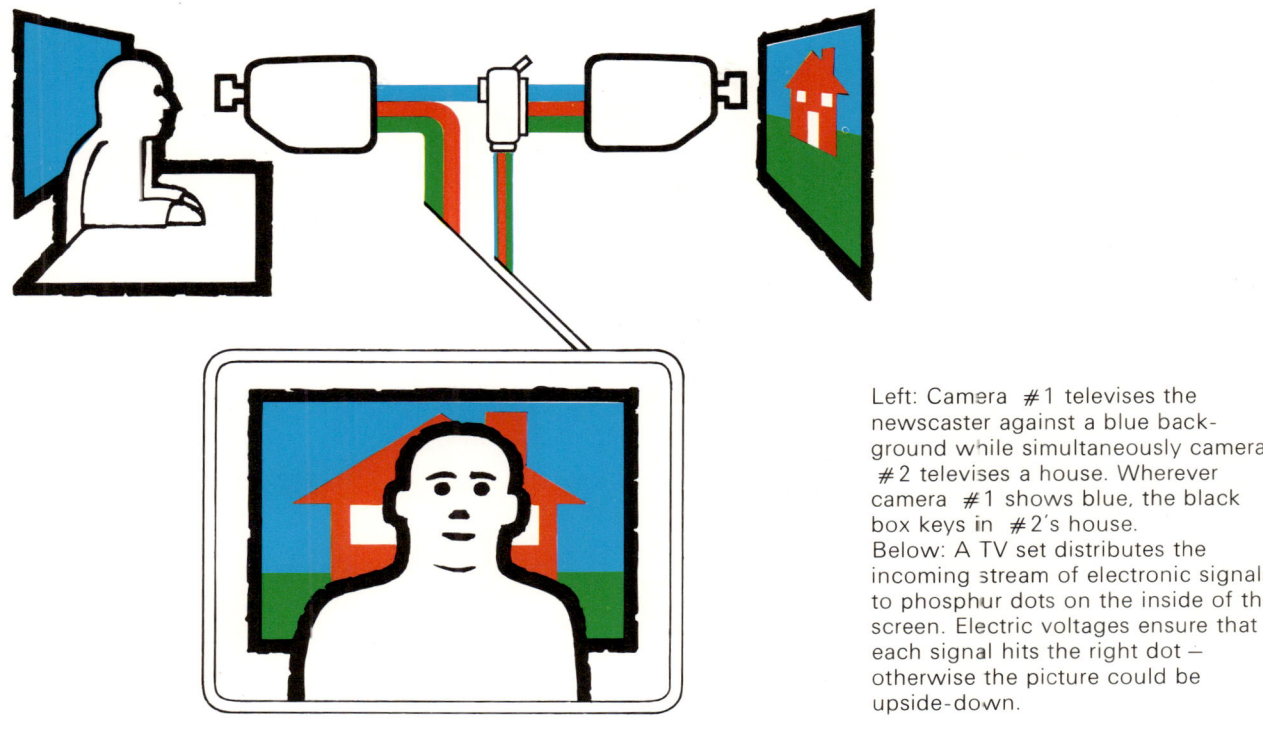

Left: Camera #1 televises the newscaster against a blue background while simultaneously camera #2 televises a house. Wherever camera #1 shows blue, the black box keys in #2's house.
Below: A TV set distributes the incoming stream of electronic signals to phosphur dots on the inside of the screen. Electric voltages ensure that each signal hits the right dot — otherwise the picture could be upside-down.

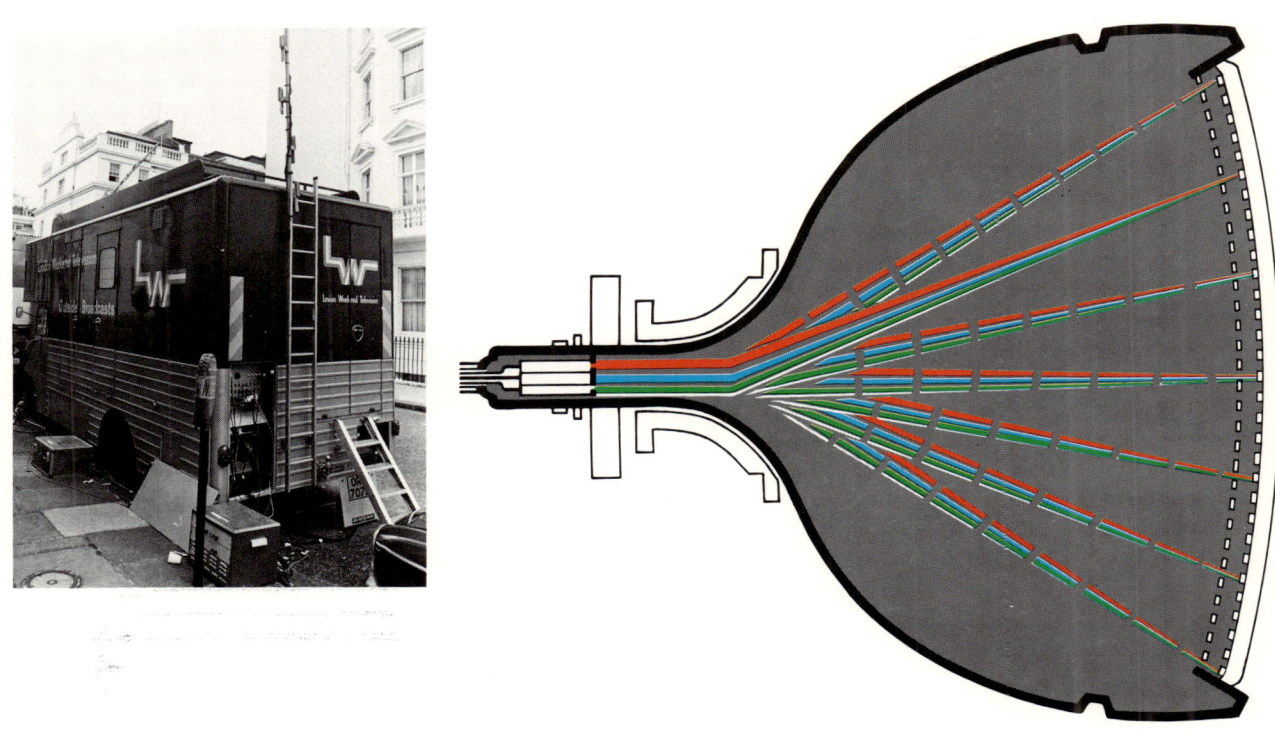

Inside a TV studio

Let us go into a TV station and, bypassing the glossy reception area and executive offices, head for the guts of the business, the studios and control rooms, to see how a studio works. But first we must check that the studio is not in use. If it is, a red light above the door will be flashing 'ON AIR'. If it is empty, enter. And be prepared for a few surprises.

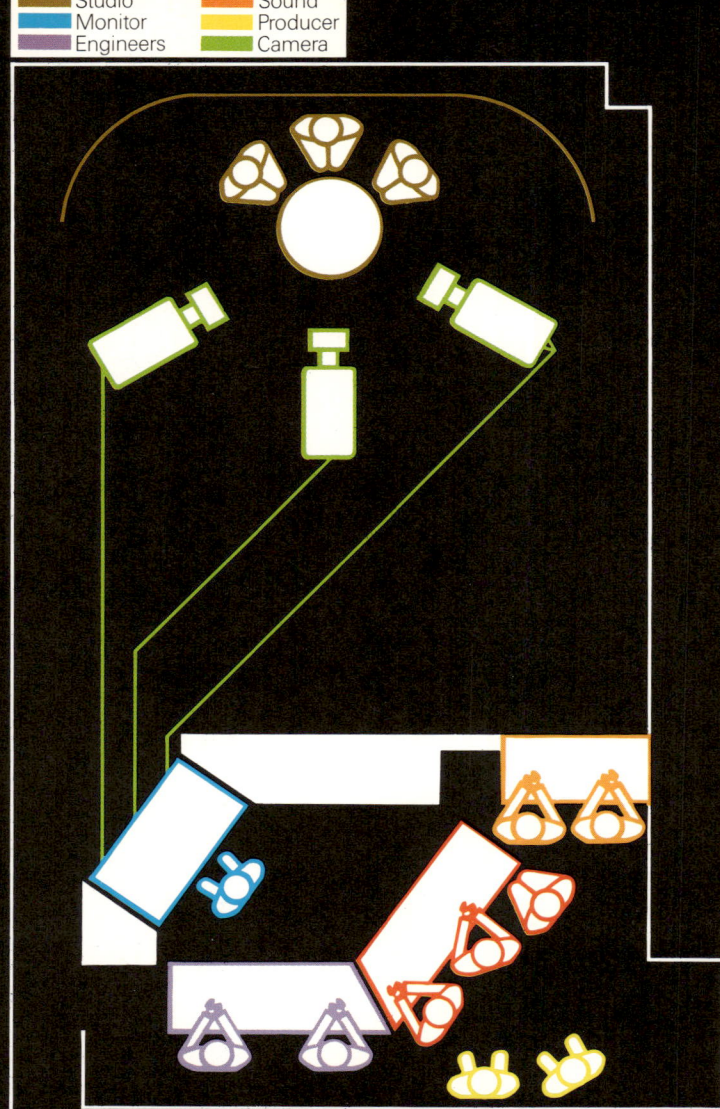

Colour Key:
- Studio
- Monitor
- Engineers
- Director
- Sound
- Producer
- Camera

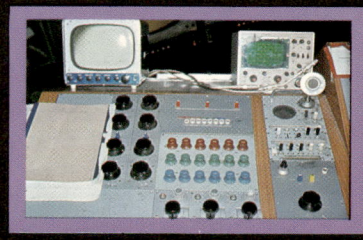

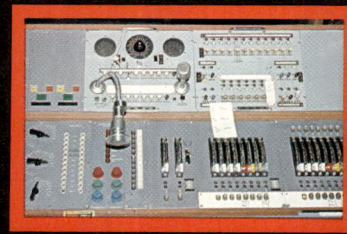

Studio TV: 1960 (above) and 1974 (right).

A television studio is a workshop. The glamorous, colourful studio set that you have seen on the screen is an artificial and temporary illusion. A real studio is a drab, grey, cold and cluttered place. But like a workshop its apparent mess and clutter probably hides an efficient and sophisticated lay-out.

TV studios vary between three different shapes and sizes. The most common has three or four cameras facing a simple backcloth. Medium-sized studios can include an audience. The director usually puts one camera at either side of the stage and one at the back of the audience. Larger studios, usually used for drama, have four or more sets arranged around the studio's edge or interlocking into each other in the middle.

Let us look more closely at the simplest of the three. The three cameras, mounted on hydraulic dollies (a kind of trolley) to allow fast and smooth tracking, will dominate the centre. They will be enveloped in yards of straggling cable. Above there are rows and rows of lights clustered together so closely that they hide the ceiling; to the left and right, more lights on telescopic stands; between them, the sound equipment.

The floor will be of hard rubber to deaden all sounds. Everything, floor included, will be painted dark grey. Around the edges the studio crew will have stored everything from last night's titles to spare bulbs.

The studio is helpless without the gallery (or control room). In it, the director sits at a bank (or console) of switches, dials and lights and the all-important monitor screens. There will be one monitor for each camera, one for the live transmission picture and one for the preview picture. The console contains all the 'cut' buttons and mixing slides.

The director sits alongside two engineers, who check the equipment, a sound recordist, and his production team. His main link with the studio crew is through two-way telephone cable to the headphones worn by practically everyone. He can speak either to the floor manager (who is the director's representative on the studio floor) or to individual cameramen. He can also use the studio's main PA system to speak to everyone.

The studio comes alive when a programme is being made; when the red light flashes 'On Air'. Let us go into the gallery and watch *Sunday Rap*, a typical discussion programme, being put together and transmitted. David Lloyd, the producer, will give us some background details. His 30-minute programme goes out once a week around 11 pm. He heads a permanent team of five (in order of seniority): assistant producer; two researchers; a PA; and a secretary. He also hires freelance reporters for particular stories.

David, with an eye on his budget (late-night chat shows cannot be generous) and with a healthy desire for an easy life, likes to decide a rough format of each programme well in advance of transmission. But he also likes to keep every programme flexible enough to accommodate last-minute items. About a fortnight before transmission he holds an informal pre-production meeting with the assistant producer, the researchers, the PA and a reporter who has been asked to provide some ideas.

In the fourteen days' run-up to recording, the production team will be constantly modifying their original ideas, changing the programme's order, and adding new items. Some ideas that sounded marvellous in the early meetings have to be rejected because nobody can think of a way of encapsulating them in a five-minute studio discussion. Other ideas may stay because they are more filmable. The programme looks like having a spare five minutes, and there is a strong possibility that the producer will use an interview that was recorded two months ago. It is not topical and can be used at any time.

David Lloyd will record most of the programme in the studio on videotape (VT). One item, which includes pictures of a nearby hotel, will be shot on film and transferred to tape.

Ten days before transmission the freelance reporter (who had the original idea), one researcher (who researched it), a director, a PA and a film crew go out on a day's location filming. The director could be the programme producer, the assistant producer, the studio director or (less likely) a researcher or an outside director.

Whatever he normally does, on location he is the director. The reporter will interview two or three people who live near the hotel (the researcher has found three suitable people but they may only have time for two). The film crew, delivered by the station's central film pool, consists of two cameramen, two sound recordists, and two lighting men. It seems a lot and it is, but the local film union will not allow its members to work in smaller groups. They will film all day and probably shoot about six rolls of film each of 10 minutes, giving a total time of 60 minutes.

The film director will ensure that his film is developed, edited and dubbed (ie, married to a sound track) in time for transmission. At each stage, he uses the station's central film labs, cutting rooms and dubbing room. He cuts the film down from 60 minutes to 9 minutes. A shooting ratio, that is, of 60:9 or 6:1 which will be acceptable both to his producer (whose budget has to pay for the original film stock) and his own sense of professional efficiency.

In the final few days' run-up to transmission, David Lloyd confirms the programme running order with his team and the studio director. They will produce each item separately; the last item, for instance, may be recorded first. All four items will come together as a programme only once – during transmission.

Transmission day arrives. The programme is scheduled for 11 pm. The production team arrives around 10 in the morning. They will not leave the building until after midnight. Probably because of the ritual of 'hospitality' drinks for themselves and their guests, not till 1 am the next morning.

At 10.30 am the PA contacts the people in the video-tape control room and tells them the final schedules. She asks them to be ready to record the various items of the programme during the day and to play back when asked (for rehearsal) and at 11 pm (for transmission). She also asks them to prepare a videotape recorder (VTR) to record the actual transmission. They reply that they will need two tapes (VTa and VTb) for the four items, and will prepare two VTRs to record transmission. The second one will stand by in case of failure.

She agrees and starts the business of getting the four items on to the tapes. First, she asks for the 9-minute film to be re-recorded on VTa (she could arrange for a tele-cine machine to convert the film to tape, but prefers to pre-record on tape). This part is easy. The rest must await the arrival of Peter Willings, the studio director. He arrives at 3 pm, as planned, and starts a practically continuous 9-hour session of rehearsal and recording, item by item.

First he rehearses the cameramen in their positions, shots and times. As he watches the picture on his three monitors he rehearses his own cutting. Meanwhile the sound engineer checks sound levels and the video engineers check the video signals for any technical faults (especially colour faults since the cameramen's view-finders, being in black-and-white, do not reveal them). He may make one or two dry runs (ie, without performers) to synchronize the crew and equipment.

Let us concentrate on one particular item: a studio discussion between the programme presenter (John Green) and a guest (Terence O'Rourke). Peter arranges

Below: lighting the set of BBC2's classic serial, *Vanity Fair*.

his cameras in the classic half-circle in front of the set. Camera One gives a medium close-up (MCU) of John Green, Camera Two gives a similar shot of Terence O'Rourke and Camera Three gives an 'establishing' shot of the whole scene: the backcloth, both speakers, and the table. The director will move Cameras One and Two *in* for headshots and *out* for mid-shots. He could go right in but rightly believes that a shot of a talking head without a neck, let alone a body, is best left to stylized drama productions.

He has decided to record the Green/O'Rourke item last of all. At 8.30 the two speakers come into the studio. John Green talks to John O'Rourke about the impending interview, or the weather, or what they had for breakfast. It does not matter: the crew are only testing the sound levels and the lights. The main direction of the discussion will have been decided beforehand by David Lloyd and the researcher. The presenter's routine contribution is usually limited to changes in style and vocabulary to

Behind the scenes in a TV studio: the sound recordist checks the microphones sound balance.

suit his own delivery (though every presenter works in a different way, and the greater their experience the greater the originality of their own contribution).

As Green and O'Rourke chat, it becomes clear that they share a genuine interest in their subject and that O'Rourke is both articulate and entertaining. The engineers signal that everything is OK. John Green and the researcher take their guest back to the hospitality room for a drink and a final chat. The studio director does a final check. In the gallery the waiting production team turn their monitors to watch a knockabout comedy on the rival channel.

At 9 pm the studio is ready. John Green and Terence O'Rourke return to their chairs. The make-up girl looks at them both suspiciously and dabs them both on the forehead. Perhaps the studio lamps were making them sweat. Perhaps she just felt like doing something.

The PA speaks to the VTR operators several floors below: 'Stand by VTR.' They are not ready – another two or three minutes. John Green mentally runs through his introduction. The cameramen gaze into space. The VTR men give a bleep; they are ready. The director asks the floor manager, 'Ready studio?' He is and he could have said so; the studio microphones would have picked up his voice and relayed it to the gallery. Instead, he looks up and nods. The PA sees him and says 'Run VTR' which means start recording. When the VT picture stabilizes (it takes about two seconds) the director tells his floor manager to tell John Green to start.

The actual recording is comparatively straightforward. John Green asks O'Rourke most of the expected questions and some unexpected ones. He shows the expected wide knowledge of O'Rourke's own subject (the researcher who briefed him feels smugly content) and a surprisingly wide knowledge of an unrehearsed subject, Britain's defence budget (which pleases David Lloyd even more). A presenter has to have the ability to stimulate and control a revealing discussion in just seven minutes; the ability to be briefed on what his guests specialize in; and the ability to cope with sudden challenges and questions. John Green seems to have all three.

The recording continues. In the gallery the studio director goes through his planned sequence of cuts. To his left, the assistant video engineer is constantly switching from camera to camera to check that the pictures are technically adequate. He checks that John's rather pale face appears the same on each camera; and that Camera Three, older than the others, does not flicker on 'green' colours.

The director has scheduled the discussion to last 6 minutes. After four minutes the floor manager holds up two fingers: two minutes to go. Then one finger: one minute to go. Then two fingers crossed: thirty seconds. Then finally he moves his hand in a clockwise circle: wind up. John Green brings the discussion to a quick and graceful close.

The recording has gone well. But the tape is not yet ready. Peter has to intercut several illustrations – diagrams – of O'Rourke's remarks. He could have done it during the discussion, but it would have tied up one and possibly two cameras and it would have been difficult, in an unscripted discussion, to cut to the diagrams at the right time. He had decided to do it later. When John and Terry had gone he asks VTR to run the newly recorded

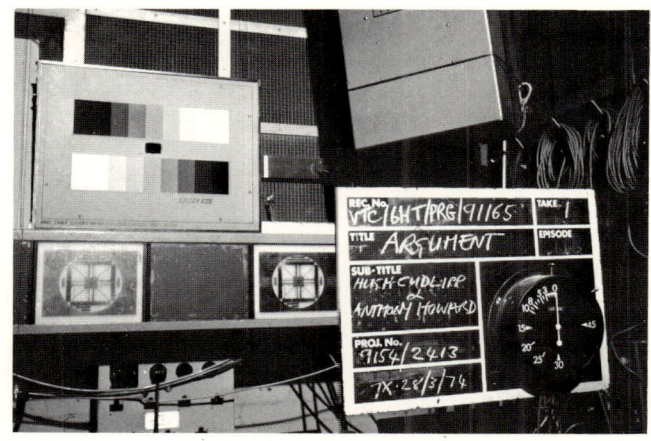

tape and watches it carefully to work out the best places to cut. Meanwhile, the studio manager re-arranges the cameras in front of two easels. That morning the researcher had pasted the illustrations on to black caption cards. The producer and Peter decided on the right order and gave the cards to the studio assistant.

Peter asks Camera One to focus on one easel and Camera Two on its neighbour. The assistant stacks the first caption and all the odd-numbered captions by the first easel, and the second and all even-numbered captions by the second easel. When they are ready, the PA runs the VT. When Terry referred to the first diagram Peter rehearses a cut to caption #1. He keeps the camera steady for a few seconds then tells the cameraman to go in for a detail of the top-right-hand corner. Then he rehearses a cut back to the VT. A few seconds later, he cuts (again, only in rehearsal) to caption #2. Meanwhile, the studio assistant has replaced caption #1 with caption #3. Peter continues with this alternate see-saw until he has included all the captions. He decides to run through the whole rehearsal twice more to make certain that the cameramen go in and out smoothly and at the right pace.

At 10.50 everybody comes back to the studio for transmission. All the items were stored on VTa or VTb except for John's brief introduction and the captions. At 10.57 an announcer from the continuity studio rings to say that the preceding programme is running 3 minutes late.

Sunday Rap's PA knows that VTa, the first tape, has to run for 30 seconds before reaching the opening titles so she asks VTR to start running it at 11.02½. In the continuity room, the announcer sees the pictures come up on his screen at 11.03 and switches across. *Sunday Rap* is on the air. Peter decides to cut from the opening titles to the studio after 35 seconds. He warns the floor manager who immediately raises his hand and watches his monitor. When Peter cuts from VTa to the studio camera +3, the floor manager brings his arm down to point at John Green. John has seen the cut out of the corner of his eye, and with the floor manager's sign for confirmation, starts his introduction: 'Good evening and welcome to another edition of *Sunday Rap* . . .'

In the gallery the PA is lining up the next item. VTa contains the starting titles, the first item and the third (the film), and the final credits. VTb contains the second and fourth items. As each item finishes, the PA repeats her count-down '5, 4, 3, 2, 1' and Peter cuts smoothly from tape to tape, ending precisely at 11.33 pm.

BRINGING BACK THE NEWS

News bulletins are television's most prestigious and serious-minded programmes. TV news is expected to be comprehensive, reliable and objective (newspapers, on the other hand, are allowed to be partisan and to make occasional mistakes). For years, the BBC was regarded by many overseas countries as the official voice of the British government. Newsreaders are regarded as sober and wise men (usually men) whose only aim is to inform.

Yet modern TV news, like modern tabloid journalism, is an incorrigible blend of journalism and entertainment. The American networks have pioneered, if that is the correct word, this modern concept of TV news as something more than a straight news service. Reuven Frank, President of NBC News until 1973, wrote: 'Every news story should, without any sacrifice of probity or responsibility, display the attributes of fiction, of drama. It should have structure and conflict, problem and denouement, rising action and falling action, a beginning, a middle and an end.' More like fiction, perhaps, than fact.

Television is most spectacular during a major national event, a sudden disaster, a crisis. It literally brings these events into the home. The results are dramatic, and permanent. American memory of November 1963 was fixed forever by the networks' television pictures of Jackie Kennedy in her bloodstained dress, the night-long reports from Bethesda, the murder of Oswald, the funeral cortège. A Briton's image of the Irish troubles is probably based on a TV picture of British troops running across a dirty Belfast street or a bombed-out shop. Vietnam 'is' a TV picture of khaki GIs stalking through tall grass or helicopters taking away wounded soldiers; or perhaps CBS's notorious film of a US soldier cutting off the ear of a peasant as a grisly memento.

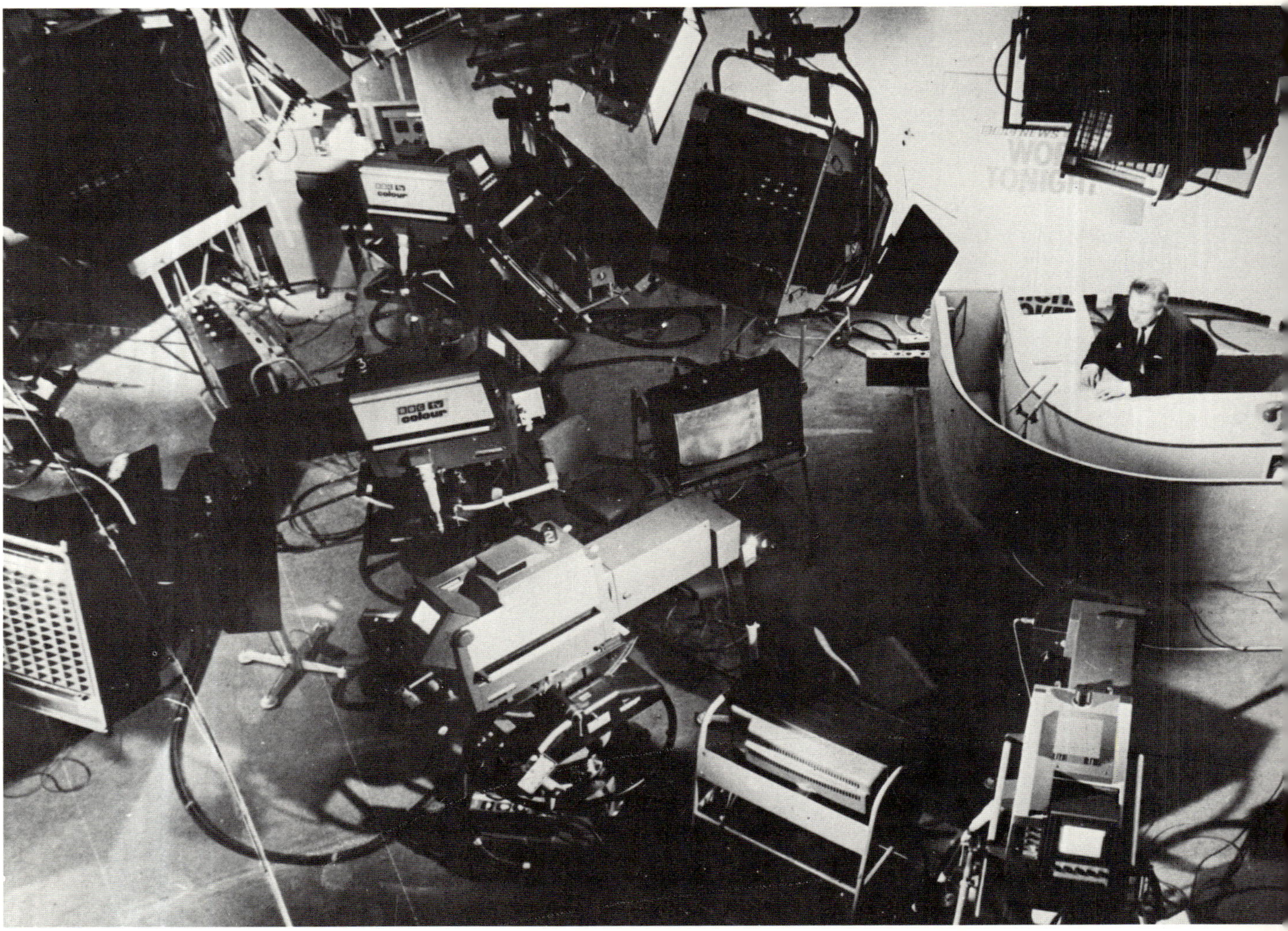

Television can provide both live coverage of sudden crises, and more sustained coverage of longer-lasting events. In February 1972 the Japanese NHK stayed on

the air for over ten hours to cover the Asama Mountain Lodge kidnapping by Rengo Sekigun. Heavy snow and freezing temperatures made the cameramen's work difficult and their pictures often flickered, but NHK stayed with it and the audience kept watching.

The more sustained TV news coverages build up tremendous visual impact. TV coverage of war (Vietnam, Nigeria, Bangladesh; and the guerrillas of America and Ulster) provokes anger, controversy and bewilderment.

The first TV war was Vietnam. The start of active

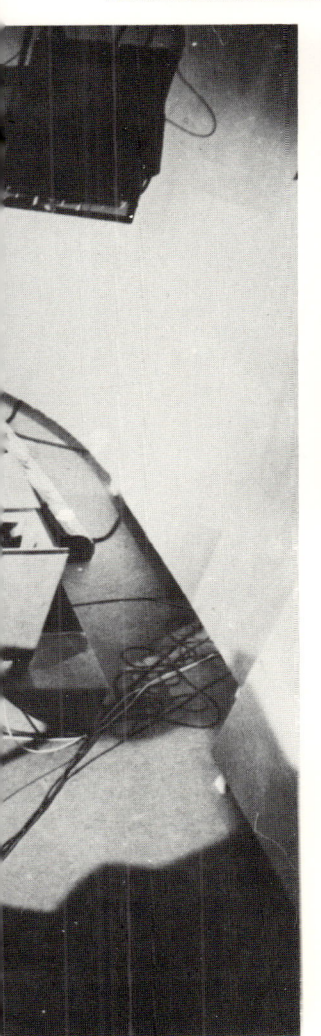

People who read the news: Kenneth Kendall (BBC), Roger Climpson (ABC) and the late Ed Murrow (CBS); and a picture of what Don Ferguson of Visnews claims is the only universal news story: "a polar bear and her baby". If the BBC studio, left, looks odd, it's because BBC news uses no studio cameramen. Everything is remote-controlled.

American involvement (US troops were officially allowed to 'take positive action in the military sense' in June 1965) coincided with CBS's first colour transmissions and the first Asia/American satellite link. Previous battlefields had remained distant: unseen and unknown. The British campaign in Burma, for example, although bloody and tortuous, remained an almost local event. But Vietnam became famous. The three US networks reported the day's battles, or the day's lack of battles, almost every night, and in 'living colour'. The American audience (and the British and French audiences) became intimately and painfully aware of Vietnam's battlelines, its towns and villages, its highways and railway bridges and its people. Some cynics said that the landscape of Vietnam became as familiar and predictable as the scenery of *Bonanza* or *Gunsmoke*. The final impression, however, was more disturbing.

The networks' TV pictures made Americans feel more involved in, but more reluctant to support, such a series of apparently haphazard endless actions. The director of CBS News in Washington, William Small, has suggested that 'TV coverage of Vietnam showed a terrible truth . . . that was cardinal to the disillusionment of Americans with this war and the destruction of Lyndon Johnson's term of office'.

The news bulletins of the 1950s were much more modest. They were shorter (15 minutes in both Britain and America), more formal and more dependent on the words. Few stories were fully illustrated. The story of TV news is one of increasing independence and professionalism; a more journalistic and entertaining presentation; and more and better news film.

The BBC's first TV news bulletins owed more to the Corporation's sense of dignity and its radio tradition than to any concept of TV. The BBC newsreaders were never seen on camera, because the Head of News, a strangely cautious and rigid New Zealander called Tahu Hole, believed that their personalities might colour the stories. So the newsreaders read their scripts over a succession of still photographs, maps and the occasional film.

The content, too, was restricted. The BBC's licence prohibited it from 'expressing any opinion on current affairs or on matters of public policy'. This was thought to outlaw scoops and in practice the BBC seldom announced anything unless Buckingham Palace or Fleet Street had said it first. The BBC was also forbidden (until 1956) to discuss any parliamentary matter for a fortnight before and during the relevant parliamentary debate. The BBC was thus reduced to supplying a sort of pictorial supplement to the news; and the pictures were often amateurish and dull. Robert Dougall, the doyen of BBC newsreaders who retired in 1973, has described the early bulletins as 'colourless, longwinded and dull . . . perhaps it would be kinder to draw a veil over those first growing pains of television news'.

Then in 1955, two weeks before Associated Rediffusion opened Britain's first commercial station, the BBC threw caution to the winds and allowed its newsreaders to be seen. They wore dinner jackets, of course, but they were otherwise revealed as normal. The next year, after a few tussles, the 14-day rule was lifted and, under the leadership of a journalist, Hugh Greene (later Director-General), the BBC's news service became one of the world's best.

ITV had a similarly troubled boyhood until in 1967 the IBA compelled all the fourteen ITV companies to carry a simultaneous national news programme, ITN's *News at Ten*. This managed to combine sharp reporting with entertaining commentary, and became one of the country's favourite programmes.

Walter Cronkite of CBS, below, is the USA's most famous and respected newsman; but outside North America, he's hardly known. Left, two BBC newscasters: Robert Dougall and Richard Baker.

Left: Andrew Gardiner and Reginald Bosanquet, two ITN newscasters, discuss the bulletin they will have to read. ABC's news "menu", above, has its own graphic language of Nixonomics, Break-In, Drought and Crisis.

News at Ten was partly modelled on American news. In 1959 the FCC had lifted the awkward Equal Time restriction, and in 1963, after some painful juggling with the relative merits of ratings, prestige and advertisement revenue, CBS expanded its *Evening News with Walter Cronkite* to 30 minutes. NBC's *Huntley-Brinkley Report* followed within a week. Nielsen has reported that from 1959 to 1963 public-service broadcasting almost doubled. Since then, the networks have been intent on consolidating their regular services and shown little interest in expansion.

The more professional and more flexible news services of the 1960s went hand-in-hand with several new technical innovations. Editors began to insist, first, on their reporters working more closely with the film crew, and vice versa, so that the words and the pictures matched each other. At the same time, they began to exploit the camera's own ability to report, and cameramen began to shoot news film that was more revealing and more memorable than the words. They shortened the tedious chain of developing-viewing-editing-dubbing from days to hours. They bought cheaper and lighter vidicon cameras and Nagra recorders and they insisted on replacing movie-size 35 mm film with the handier 16 mm.

But even 16 mm film is cumbersome and expensive. The fastest news operation cannot process and edit film in less than 1½ hours (dubbing adds at least another 45 minutes), and the finished film is not always satisfactory. High-Speed Ektachrome is especially unreliable in its colour values.

At present, a news editor prepares the day's schedules knowing that every bit of film must be brought back to the station's labs (by despatch rider or car) and processed. If he uses videotape he can miss out the second stage. But someone has to get the tape back to the station.

A fully electronic system removes both stages. The crew can record electronically (i.e., with TV cameras, not film cameras) and use a portable microwave transmitter to send the pictures direct to the station. There, the news editor can either record the signal on videotape or re-transmit it live.

CBS started this 'live mode' television in 1972 in Philadelphia and all three networks now use it regularly. New York, with its jungle of skyscrapers, presents special difficulties. CBS engineers have to send a specially strengthened signal and hope that it will bounce its way around the city until it finds the CBS antenna. WCBS's live after-the-show reviews at Sardi's, one of the station's most cultured and literary programmes, thus reaches its viewers after being bounced off the walls of the city's tenements.

This bit of technological gadgetry and the lighter and more flexible 16-mm cameras could make TV news more up to date and more adventurous. But two problems remain. TV news is much clumsier than radio; the TV equipment is heavier than radio's, and TV pictures cannot yet be delivered along a telephone line. Secondly, TV news bulletins are more superficial than newspapers and magazines. The average 30-minute TV news bulletin has fewer words than the front page of the *New York Times* or the London *Times*. Television's strength, and its weakness, is its visual impact, which convinces and confuses, reveals and misleads, with equal authority and equal facility.

THE MIDDLE EAST WAR OCTOBER 1973

The Middle East war of October 1973 tested all the major news organizations: the three American networks, the BBC and ITN, the French ORTF, the German ARD and Japanese NHK.

Newspapers can advertise their successes: 'Our Man in Tel Aviv' or 'Tom Hindley, First Man in War-Torn Damascus'. But TV is more modest. A TV station may spend thousands getting a man to Tel Aviv and thousands getting his pictures back by satellite. But it will never say so. So few people knew if CBS or NBC provided the better coverage, and even fewer if CBS was better than NHK.

This chapter will tell the story of ITN's coverage of the Middle East war; the story reveals the resources and skills of a major news station. Ask any editor the worst possible time for a major news story to break and he will probably say Saturday afternoon. News is a tricky business at the best of times. You cannot plan for it or budget for it except in the most general terms. But some times make it more tricky than others.

The Middle East war started on Saturday 6 October. ITN, situated in the heart of London's rag trade, heard the first rumours during the morning. John Mahoney, the duty foreign news editor, soon realized that the fighting was serious. A girl assistant was telephoning their Tel Aviv stringer when she got dramatic confirmation: she heard, in the background, the wailing of an air-raid siren. ITN had to do two things fast. First, get some reporters and a film crew into the war zone; second, book some satellite time to get their pictures back.

They started with the reporters. The commercial airline schedules, of course, are the first casualties of a modern war. Israel, Egypt and Syria had already closed their airports to all normal traffic. But the British were lucky. There was an El Al plane at Heathrow Airport, scheduled to take off at 4 pm. ITN suspected that it

would fly to Israel within the day (though they thought 4 pm rather optimistic) because the Israelis would want to use it as a troop carrier. They managed to book one seat.

The satellite proved easier. ITN's main bulletin is the 30-minute *News at Ten*. ITN knew that their film crews would have great difficulty in getting their films processed and ready for transmission and that they would prefer a satellite slot as near to 10 pm as possible. But they soon discovered that most of the more desirable times were fully booked. Spain, for instance, has several regular bookings for sending programmes to South America and the Canary Islands. And she was determined to keep them. On the first night, when Israel wanted to transmit pictures which disproved Egypt's claim that the Israelis had touched off the war, Spain insisted on sending a 2-hour bullfight to South America. A few days later Spain took three crucial hours to relay a tennis match to the Canary Islands. But ITN was able to book a daily 10-minute slot for a month.

Back at Heathrow, the El Al plane was still on the tarmac. ITN in fact was not altogether sorry. Many civil passengers had decided to cancel their bookings and ITN were able to book five more seats. The plane eventually took off at 4 pm on Sunday, 24 hours late, with a large press contingent. ITN had producer David Phillips, reporters Gerald Seymour and Michael Nicholson, cameraman Chris Faulds, sound recordist John Soldini and film editor John Harwood.

Another ITV company, meanwhile, had had an astonishing stroke of luck. John Fielding, a reporter for Thames' *This Week* current affairs programme, happened to be in Tel Aviv on another story. And so *Weekend World*, ITV's Sunday morning programme, was able to get a first-hand, live-by-satellite, report.

By Sunday night, ITN had got reporters and a film

ITN crews shot thousands of feet of news-film throughout the 17-day war. This page and the next two show a fraction of it — both pictures that were transmitted and some that were not.

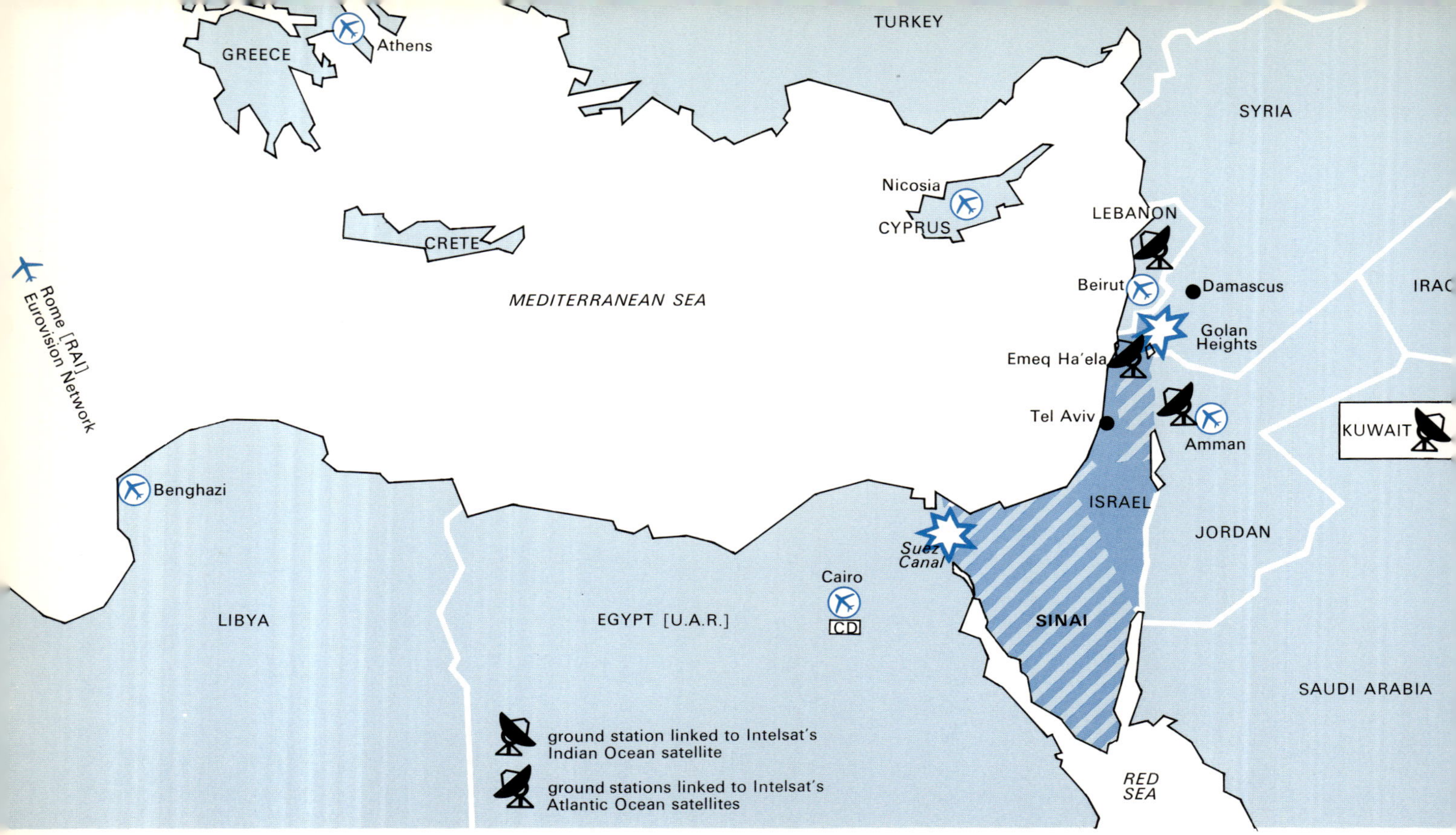

The war-zone – for both the military and the TV reporters. ✈ show airports, 📡 show satellite earth stations, and ✡ mark the two main battlefronts.

Left: more ITN newsfilm. The soldier in the bottom picture is painting instructions on the road for an approaching convoy.

crew into Tel Aviv. Egypt was a harder nut to crack. Cairo airport was closed. The nearest alternative was Benghazi in Libya – 1,000 miles across the desert. Undeterred, ITN's Robert Southgate flew to Benghazi and caught a bus to Cairo. The bus took thirty hours to get there. Richard Lindley and Tony Summers of the BBC took the same route, spending two days to cross the desert in buses and cars.

During Sunday and Monday the world's press – producers, editors, reporters, cameramen, soundmen, PAs – tried to infiltrate the war zones with as much speed and energy as the most determined guerrilla. Norman Rees of ITN flew to Beirut and then drove to Damascus to cover the Syrian front. The BBC's Keith Graves and Bill Baglin flew to Nicosia in Cyprus, to Athens and then managed to get to Israel. Larry Harris and Bill Nicol waited at Heathrow for 30 hours before flying to Amman. Others followed Southgate, Lindley and Summers across the Libyan desert.

ITN's first major war bulletin was Monday night's *News at Ten*. By then, ITN had reporters on both the Sinai and Golan fronts. The bulletin carried news film and voice reports from both fronts and some of Syrian Arab Television's black-and-white pictures (accompanied by SAT's proudly martial music).

By midweek, ITN and all major news stations had established firm bases throughout the war zones. ITN had 19 people there. The HQ was Tel Aviv with one producer, two PAs, three film editors and two reporters. They also had a reporter and a film crew in Egypt, Syria and Jordan. Two news agencies supplied further stories: the international UPI-ITN and Middle East Media.

Meanwhile the battlefronts changed daily; and the reports, rumours and gossip much more often. In the first few days Egypt swept across the Suez Canal and the Syrians stormed down from the Golan Heights. The battle on Sinai was especially fierce, bloody and confusing and without quarter. Neither Egypt nor Israel, during the climactic three days, were saying anything.

The problem, throughout the war, was secrecy. Cairo was reputed to have over 400 foreign journalists and thirty foreign film crews. Their contact was the Ministry of Information and the Ministry, according to ITN, had 'total goodwill', but the ministry could not persuade the Army and without the Army's permission nothing happened. No film crews were allowed to film in the streets (reporters had to speak their 'stand-ups' on hotel balconies) and only three crews were allowed near the front.

The other Arab countries were even less friendly. Syria refused all film permits except for bomb damage in Damascus (which had an obvious propaganda value) and the Golan Heights were permanently out of bounds. The Syrians and several other governments continually offered Western crews their own rather boring and badly scratched black-and-white film, and were continually surprised when the Westerners refused it. Jordan did not allow Western crews to film at all. ITN and the more experienced crews, nevertheless, did manage to find and film the action during the three weeks. The final problem, of course, was getting the film and voice reports past the censor and out of the country.

The censors were fairly straightforward. Reporters and film editors knew roughly what the local censor would allow and what he would cut. They might risk a 'dodgy' statement, but only seldom since late changes were embarrassing, awkward and time-consuming. They would never try to cheat. The reprisals are swift and simple and unanswerable.

The final stage is transmission. Since the 1967 war Israel, Lebanon and Jordan had built ground stations linked to Intelsat's Atlantic satellites. Egypt had not built one, and she had described a temporary portable station as 'too expensive'. Getting the pictures home was easier (in theory, anyway) than in most other war zones. But it was still difficult.

Israel was the most efficient and the quickest. The Israel Broadcasting Authority provided a one day turnaround for film processing and transmission. ITN film crews could drive from Tel Aviv to the Sinai front in five hours (the Golan Heights were slightly closer). They could film until 2 pm, drive back fast to Tel Aviv, process the film on the IBA's sophisticated colour equipment (two hours) and send their pictures to the IBA ground station at Emeq Ha'ela.

The Arabs were much less cooperative. Egypt, obviously, was the centre for news stories; and Cairo airport was closed to civil flights. Most film crews sent their films to Benghazi airport for rapid air-freighting to Rome where RAI injected them into the Eurovision network. The alternative route sounds better but had several snags. The Egyptians occasionally flew a diplomatic plane from Cairo to London, Rome, Frankfurt, or other European centres, and some Egyptian officials were willing to carry film as diplomatic baggage. The flights, alas, were susceptible to last-minute changes of route and timing. ITN completely lost one shipment.

The other Arab countries were also awkward. Reporters and crews based in Damascus, the Syrian capital, had only a 60-mile drive to the Golan Heights. But Syria, like Egypt, does not have a satellite station, nor any microwave circuits. So editors had to send their final film by car to the ground station at Amman, which took six hours, or westwards to Beirut, which took longer. Several American crews sent their film to Kuwait and thence to Intelsat's Indian Ocean satellite.

The problems sound immense. But ITN were able to fill their daily 10-minute satellite slot with good, up to date material, as well as sending more film by car, taxi and plane. In London, *News at Ten* kept the Middle East war as a lead story almost every night. Viewing figures were high for the first week, but unusually low for the second week. Perhaps British audiences had tired of the necessarily repetitive shots of tanks-in-the-desert and soldiers-at-rest. Perhaps, being ignorant of the problems, they thought that ITN (and the BBC, whose figures also fell) had not got close enough to the fighting, the horror and the suffering. Or, perhaps, *too* close. The figures, of course, may be unrelated to the war stories.

The pressures of reporting a war are immense. Few TV people were physically hurt, although Mike Nicholson of ITN was buzzed by two Syrian pilots while driving to the Golan Heights and his car crashed; he had to wear a neck brace. And two cameramen from the BBC and NBC received shrapnel wounds and went to hospital.

The real pressures are more complicated. The Red Cross, for instance, complained of some US and local news film of prisoners of war. They said the film 'made a show of the prisoners and humiliated them and therefore broke the Geneva Convention. Most broadcasters totally disagreed, saying that cameras could not create humiliation where none was present before; and that, with local news film, many families would be relieved to know their relatives were alive.

The broadcasters had a good point, since Israel and most Arab countries tune in to each others' programmes. One film crew had harrowing experience of this interchange of programmes. They were invited by the Syrian government to film a captured Israeli pilot. Since film in Syria was short, they accepted. When they arrived, they discovered that the pilot was badly hurt and that the Syrians wanted them to film some doctors operating on him. The crew was rather reluctant but filmed a short sequence. Back in Tel Aviv a distraught Israeli, who had seen their film on TV, came to their hotel. 'I have a brother who was shot down. Was that him?' The crew could not be sure, and were reluctant to raise false hopes. Later, the father and sister turned up, but the crew could not comfort them.

Worldwide television proved itself expert during the war at what Variety rather callously called: 'Instant Replay for World Screens'. Certainly, people felt deeply involved. A New York telethon (a fund-raising marathon) on 21 October raised $3,500,000 in 4½ hours and another $500,000 after the show closed. It was a record.

PRODUCING DRAMA FOR TELEVISION

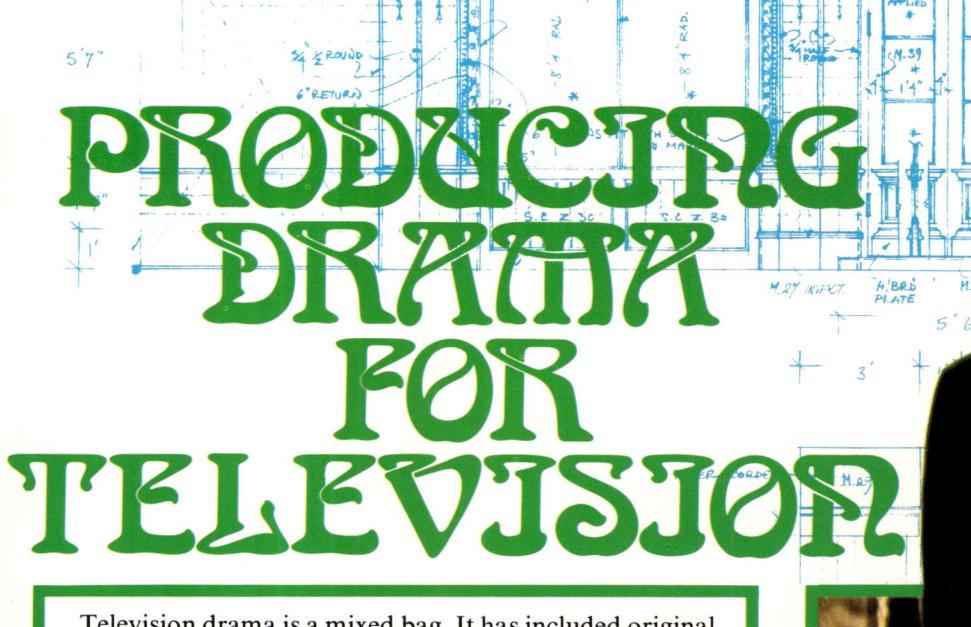

Television drama is a mixed bag. It has included original plays like *Dial M for Murder* (which was adapted for the stage and movies); a studio production of *Hamlet*; a 26-part dramatization of *The Forsyte Saga*; an unscripted original play with amateur actors, like *Hard Labour*; an anthology series about Love; a drama-documentary like *Cathy Come Home*, about homelessness; and ABC's four-times-a-week 15-minute serial, *Bellbird*, which features the adventures, so called, of a mythical Australian country town.

TV drama has always been difficult to define. At first, nobody could decide whether TV drama was theatre, or the movies – or neither? The first television play (produced in Schenectady in 1928 and not, as the BBC believe, in London in 1930) solved this Gordian knot with a compromise. The first experiments in TV drama were radio drama with pictures.

Slowly, drama directors began to discover television. They learned how to handle cameras and they explored the aesthetics of cutting and mixing. Writers began to write proper camera scripts. Actors learned how to perform in front of the unwieldy TV cameras. In the mid-1950s Paddy Chayevsky and Rod Serling (in America) and Michael Barry (in London) began to produce plays that, although dependent on the traditional theatre, were recognizably of television.

The American honeymoon did not last long. Hollywood decided to treat the TV networks as movie networks. They used their massive resources to churn out slick and syrupy series (like *Peyton Place*) that engulfed the adolescent stirrings of the real thing. The single TV play had a brief revival around 1966/7 but is now nearly extinct. Some TV stations are nowadays content to produce only slick made-for-TV movies and soap operas which are cheap in money, resources and imagination. Britain's BBC and ITV stations are almost unique in the range and depth of their regular, thoughtful and often provocative TV drama. Each week, they transmit several single plays (though fewer than in the 1960s), series and serials. They do produce failures, such as the BBC's *The Pallisers* (a lavish attempt to reincarnate their *Forsyte Saga*) and numerous series which concentrate on quick gags at the expense of character, plot, humour and meaning.

But British television has produced, and exported, a number of successes. The story really starts in 1958 when ABC, part of the ITV network, hired the abrasive energetic Canadian Sidney Newman to produce their weekly Armchair Theatre. He immediately started to produce hard hitting, exciting and provocative plays about modern British life.

The BBC's Michael Barry continued, for a few years, to produce the BBC's traditional mixture of classics, adaptations and serials until, in 1961, he sensed the new climate and resigned. In 1962, his assistant, Elwyn Jones produced the first *Z Cars* and the BBC took the logical step of asking Newman to be their Head of Drama. There, he joined an explosive collection of talented producers, script editors, directors and writers who shared his enthusiasm for drama that was fast-moving and relevant; they included Troy Kennedy Martin, Herbert Wise, Tony Garnett, Andrew Osborne, James MacTaggart, Alun Owen, John McGrath, John Hopkins, Dennis Potter, David Mercer, John Bowen, William Trevor, Jim Allen and Jeremy Sandford.

Sidney Newman was notorious for his slogans: 'Our greatest strength is our ignorance'; and 'I don't want writers, I want people who want to say something'. But he knew that his first duty was to entertain: 'Tell the writer that if his play has a message, the characters mustn't know it.' Newman was determined to make the best of his writers, and his directors and cameramen too.

Sidney Newman left the BBC in 1967 and, after two years, returned to Canada. He had been midwife to a new kind of TV drama. His credits include the BBC's regular Wednesday Play, *The Forsyte Saga*, *The Avengers*, *Dr Who*, *Cathy Come Home* and Harold Pinter's first TV

play, *A Night Out*. Sidney Newman's productions were not exclusively highbrow or lowbrow plays, but they were definitely television plays. Newman and his colleagues had shown that TV drama did exist as a unique form. It was not the movies (although it was often shot on film and borrowed film techniques). It was not theatre (although TV producers often adapted stage plays). And it had left the swaddling clothes of radio far behind.

TV drama was simple and small where the movies were large in scale and budget; intimate where they were grand; tight where they were loose; and homely where they were momentous. Every TV station, of course, could not resist the temptation to produce the occasional big-budget spectacular. In 1970 the BBC's huge success with its *Six Wives of Henry VIII* and its imitative *Elizabeth R.* (1971) started a reactionary wave of historical and nostalgic costume drama. The genre had a few successes, but they were submerged in the general feeling of predictable frivolity. One of the most famous TV spectaculars, and one of the worst, was the BBC's *War and Peace* (1972).

But increasingly the better TV producers realized that TV drama had its own strengths and weaknesses, and they set out to exploit them. Most of the more adventurous producers concentrated on two areas. The mavericks, like Tony Garnett and his colleagues, used ordinary people and ordinary situations to create drama that was rough hewn, unpredictable and fiercely political. Other producers concentrated on translating almost anything – ancient legends, 1920 short stories or even their own original ideas – into a form fit for 1970 TV. Their sources were infinitely varied, but the results were remarkably similar in form, and they were all directly relevant to the ordinary lives of the viewers. Two outstanding examples of the first are Tony Garnett's *Blooming Youth* and *Hard Labour*, in which Garnett and the mostly young or inexperienced cast combined to write the script and create the play. Of the second, Derek Granger's *Country Matters* (adaptations of short stories), John Finch's *Sam* (a serial based on his own upbringing as a miner's son) and Richard Bates' *Helen: A Woman of Today* (an original serial about a couple, with children, who slowly and painfully divorce each other). But these memorable plays are exceptions. Most TV drama concentrates, if that is the right word, on not annoying the viewer, and does not attempt to shock him or possibly educate him.

Below: Bryan Marshall and Barbara Ewing in Granada's brilliant adaptation, *The Little Farm*.

Far top: *Long Day's Journey Into Night* (ATV) with Laurence Olivier; far bottom: *Helen – A Woman of Today* (LWT); middle: *No Trams to Lime Street* (BBC). Overleaf: *The Six Wives of Henry VIII* (BBC).

UPSTAIRS DOWNSTAIRS the house that Jean built

One of Britain's most successful series is *Upstairs Downstairs*, a 'serious' factual drama series about a household in Edwardian London. The point of the series is that it deals equally with 'upstairs' and 'downstairs' – with the aristocratic Bellamy family and with their servants.

Upstairs Downstairs is successful both artistically and commercially. The first and third series won the 1971 and 1973 SFTA Award (the major British award) for the best drama series. The first three series were sold to over 20 TV stations including RTC of Canada, WGBH (Boston) and WNET (New York), and the Australian Channel 9; and, more surprisingly, to Sierra Leone, Trinidad and Yugoslavia. Sagitta, the production company, have pro-

An ad in America's *TV Guide*, left, promises everything for the first US showing of *Upstairs Downstairs*. The sequence, below, shows the series' co-creator, Jean Marsh, as Rose leaving the house.

Behind these sober faces, lurk 13 weeks of sex, intrigue, jealousy, and just plain fun.

duced nine books ranging from *Mr Hudson's Diaries* to *Mrs Bridges' Upstairs Downstairs Cookery Book*.

Upstairs Downstairs had some unusual origins. Jean Marsh and Eileen Atkins, two actresses, were sunbathing by the side of the luxurious Riviera swimming pool of Lord Glenavy (better known as Patrick Campbell) and thinking how they could become as rich as their host. Jean Marsh had been born the daughter of a Cockney housemaid. Eileen Atkins' father had been an under-butler. The answer, they decided, was to generate a TV series about a large aristocratic household in Victorian London (later changed to Edwardian) showing how life upstairs, lived by Lord Glenavy and his kind, contrasted with life downstairs lived by their own parents. Together they wrote a synopsis and enough basic plots for thirteen episodes. They contacted Sagitta, a London TV agency, and in the summer of 1969 sold them 50 per cent of the rights in the still unwritten series.

In December London Weekend, one of Britain's new ITV stations, decided to buy the series. John Hawkesworth of Sagitta was appointed producer.

Both John Hawkesworth and his script editor, Alfred Shaughnessy, were determined to keep a tight control over the entire production. Hawkesworth wrote synopses for all the episodes indicating the style (comedy, tragedy, drama), the leading characters and the plot. Alfred

Shaughnessy worked carefully with all the writers to maintain a 'house' style.

John Hawkesworth wanted every episode to be a complete story so that casual viewers could enjoy it. He also wanted to make TV, not a movie: 'Let's remember that television is electronic theatre and not second-rate film.'

In April 1970 London Weekend scheduled *Upstairs Downstairs* for recording in the autumn and transmission the following spring. John Hawkesworth did not have much time: 'Taking October 23 as the first VTR on a two-week turn-around, we must aim at having the first six scripts delivered in draft stage for planning twelve weeks before that date. That is, by Monday August 3. This is only five weeks away so we are already short of time. We shall have to commission six writers initially and pick the best to write more plays in the series.'

He gave the crucial task of writing the first episode to the established and successful Fay Weldon. She wrote the first draft while on a fortnight's holiday in France. Alfred Shaughnessy completely rewrote the first scene and altered others. The changes were extensive, demonstrating the important role of the script editor.

Eileen Atkins, meanwhile, had made the difficult decision to leave the series just as it was finally getting off the ground. She had been offered the part of Elizabeth I in Robert Bolt's *Vivat Vivat Regina* at Chichester, and felt she could not refuse. John Hawkesworth had to find a replacement, quickly. By luck, at the SFTA Annual Awards dinner he sat next to a bright and vivacious up-and-coming actress called Pauline Collins who seemed perfect for the part. (In 1972 the same SFTA nominated Pauline Collins as Best Actress for her role in *Upstairs Downstairs*.) Fay Weldon slightly rewrote her first episode to accommodate the change. It was recorded on 11 November 1970.

The first series was a critical and ratings success. The Writers' Guild gave Fay Weldon their Best Series Script Award and the more prestigious SFTA overcame their then traditional BBC bias to give the whole series its first

Best Series Award. The viewers, too, put almost every episode into the Top Twenty. London Weekend decided to go ahead with a second series (recorded in summer 1972) and a third (autumn 1973).

The third series covered the frenetic years from 1912 to 1914. When rehearsals started, the cast had a strong sense of being part of the same family. But one member was missing. Rachel Gurney, who played Lady Marjorie Bellamy, had decided to leave. John Hawkesworth devised an ingenious exit. He put her on the *Titanic*. He also decided that Rose, the gentle and sheltered parlourmaid, should have a proposal of marriage. He asked Jeremy Paul to write a script: A Perfect Stranger.

Below: the Upstairs family. Right: preparations for recording *A Perfect Stranger*.

Right: Hudson, the butler and Mrs Bridges, the cook.

Below: Mrs Bridges, with Hudson listening, makes a point with the Bellamy family.

Left: nowadays, they would be watching television...

A Perfect Stranger

Rose looks up at her boyfriend; the bottom of the staircase can be seen in the ballroom scene on the previous page.

Jeremy Paul was one of John Hawkesworth's stable of regular writers. He had written seven previous episodes including three in the third series. He and the other regulars had overcome the problems that had faced Fay Weldon and were usually able to hit the bull's eye with their first draft. His script for A Perfect Stranger was about ten minutes too long (his last script had been ten minutes too short so he had drastically overcorrected). But, after cutting, it needed few alterations.

A Perfect Stranger tells how Rose is delivering a cake to a friend when, on the tram, an Australian accidentally damages it, introduces himself and offers to buy a new one. In the cake shop he buys Rose tea; they begin to like each other. Gregory is energetic, direct and likeable; and Rose, humble and inexperienced, is impressed and slightly overwhelmed. After a few days, Gregory asks Rose to come back with him to Australia. His boat sails in a few days. Rose cannot decide. She has been 'in service' all her life and never thought of marriage. Her fellow servants are unhelpful. They invite Gregory to tea, 'to have a look at him'. During tea, Rose suddenly decides 'I'm going'. She packs and after tearful farewells travels to the docks. But a few hours later, she returns. She says that Gregory is already married; but Mrs Bellamy, her mistress, knows that Rose has lost her nerve.

The story was a winner, a real tear-jerker, destined to plunge the sixteen million fans of Upstairs Downstairs into an agony of will she, won't she?

The man chosen to direct this plum was Christopher Hodson, another Upstairs Downstairs regular (it was his third play in the current series). Directors work on a six-week turn around, which means that they can record a new play every six weeks (the cast record a new play every two weeks).

A TV drama director has to direct two distinct processes: the technical and the artistic. The two, of course, overlap. But TV production consists of numerous fragmented activities, from finding locations to organizing the shooting schedule, which the director has to consider before he can fully explore the play's artistic content.

Chris Hodson read A Perfect Stranger on 22 October 1973. He first planned his technical strategy and he soon realized that the play had a large number of technical problems, including two location scenes at an Edwardian tea dance. Hodson and his PA scoured London for suitable places – in vain. Then he remembered Le Café de Paris in Coventry Street, where he and his wife had celebrated their first wedding anniversary (and Noël Coward had done the cabaret). A phone call revealed that the Café was still there, though heavily disguised as a Mecca dance hall. He inspected it and booked it for one day.

The third location scene was much easier: a street scene outside the Bellamy House that the Upstairs Downstairs team had done many times before. Four other scenes required special sets: the tram, the cake shop, a shipping office and a taxi interior. The last three just needed studio sets; but the tram was more complicated. It really required a moving backcloth of an Edwardian street. But not even Upstairs Downstairs expert researchers could produce any colour film of 1914 London. So the designer painted a suitable street scene on a long strip of canvas and wound it round a roller device that, when unrolled, would give the tram the appearance of moving jerkily forward.

When Chris Hodson had worked out his production strategy, he could concentrate on the words. He had four weeks, in all, before meeting the actors. He worked step by step, visualizing each scene and calculating the best way of recording it.

Meanwhile he and Martin Case, the company's casting director, had solved the major problem of casting the Australian, Gregory Wilmot. It was a difficult part. Gregory had to be lively and assertive; he also had to convince the shrewd and retiring Rose that she should go with him to Australia. The accent, too, was tricky. The script specified an Essex farmer who had spent six years in Australia. The two directors found several actors who could have won Rose but none had the right accent. Then Keith Barron became available and was chosen.

and chalk to represent the studio sets. Poles mark doorways. Battered sofas and kitchen chairs stand in for the Bellamys' elegant furniture. A round tin tray is the silver salver. A chipped biscuit tin is Mr Bellamy's cigar box.

Rehearsal is a slow business. The actors move around waiting, talking to each other, reading their lines, drinking coffee, waiting. Somewhere the director will be rehearsing a scene. A few markings on the floor, a trestle table and three poles suddenly become the kitchen. Simon Williams stops practising leg-breaks and becomes Captain Bellamy, the impetuous and arrogant master of the house (and the pitch becomes a staircase). Jean Marsh puts down a copy of *Vogue* and becomes a head house parlourmaid.

Martin Case also had to find actors for seven speaking parts, extras for 46 non-speaking parts, and five actor-musicians.

The regular *Upstairs Downstairs* team start a new play every other Saturday. They met A Perfect Stranger at a read-through on Saturday 10 November. Rehearsals started the following Monday. *Upstairs Downstairs* always read through and rehearse in the same place: the Duke of York's Barracks in Kings Road. The Barracks must have flourished in Edwardian years – especially in the troubled year of 1914. Today, it is half empty. Kings Road, as Hudson might say, has changed somewhat since those times.

The actors, all wearing casual clothes, rehearse in an enormous room. The floor is marked with sticky tape

The director concentrates, at this stage, on the basic structure of the play – on coordinating the movements of the actors and cameras. Both Chris Hodson and, of course, the resident cast, have worked on *Upstairs Downstairs* many times before so the rehearsal goes smoothly. But some apparently straightforward scenes still need several run-throughs. The director may discover that an actor's position that seemed all right on paper will actually obscure one of the cameras. Or he may decide to change a two-shot (showing two people) to a close-up or reaction shot (showing a close-up of one actor reacting to somebody else).

The director and actors rehearse from Monday to Friday. On the second Monday, Chris Hodson recorded the location scenes. He planned the day with the precision and efficiency of a military coup. He had to move 54 actors (including extras) and 20 technicians to and from two locations in the centre of London, and rehearse and record two scenes, in twelve hours from 8 am to 8.30 pm. In the morning he recorded Rose's departure outside the Bellamys' house. Then he moved to the more complicated tea dance at the Café de Paris.

A film crew had been at the Café since 10 am to prepare the two cameras and the lights. They had linked the cameras to the large outside-broadcast van (a sort of mobile control room) by snaking the cables through the windows into the kitchen and along the dance floor. Chris Hodson held two rehearsals and then recorded.

The next day everyone was back in the Duke of York's Barracks for the final two days' rehearsals. On Tuesday the technical crew joined them and on the last day everybody came: the author, the producer, the script editor and the vision mixer.

Upstairs Downstairs is recorded in London Weekend's 7,600-sq ft Studio One. The studio crew had assembled the sets on Tuesday and 'dressed' them on Wednesday. The first arrivals on Thursday were the lighting crew – at 8 am. In mid-morning Chris Hodson painstakingly started to go through every one of the play's 374 shots. He checked the camera positions, the lights, the sound levels. He checked that the PA, on his left, was herself checking every shot and keeping the cameramen on schedule and he checked that the vision mixer on his right was cutting from one camera to another at the right moment.

Camera rehearsals, like actors' rehearsals, appear slow and fragmented. Most of the time everybody seems to be waiting for someone else to do something. But long gaps are unavoidable as the director orchestrates the actors, cameras, and vision mixer in such a complicated routine. Even simple shots, again, can cause problems. In one scene Chris Hodson had hoped to shoot Gregory through the kitchen hatch. But the cameraman, after almost managing it, said it was impossible. So the camera script had to be rewritten, the lights readjusted, the microphones moved and the furniture shifted.

Chris Hodson rehearsed in the studio for a day and a half and recorded, as expected, on Friday.

Television, even during recording, never has the theatrical excitement of a stage play. There are frequent

interruptions (recording a 50-minute play takes about five hours) while the actors and cameras move from set to set and the director and PA continually check that everything is in order. They communicate through personal mikes and headsets or through the studio's own playback sound system. Instructions, questions, advice, jokes and plain irrelevancies bounce around the studio. It is like a deep millpond compared to the fast and dramatic rapids of the final edited tape.

But television has its own excitement: the professional hunt for the best recording.

The next day, the permanent actors read through the script of the next episode, quickly forgetting Rose's fling with Gregory; and the studio crew start to rehearse a variety show. But Chris Hodson and his PA are far from finished. They have to turn the studio tapes and the location tape into – they hope – a polished and exciting play.

Videotape cannot be cut and spliced like film because the video and sound signals are recorded invisibly and diagonally across its length. Instead, the VT editor plays back the original 'master' tape on one VTR and re-records the bits he wants to keep on another 'slave' tape.

The basic point of editing (to adapt Ernest Hemingway's description of good writing) is to put the best scenes in the best order. The director and editor (and their relationship is always a secret between them) contrive to create a tape which has the right *meaning* and the right *pace*. When Gregory and Rose entered the Café de Paris, for example, Chris Hodson made a succession of fast cuts to the drummer, the band, the staircase and the dance floor in a strict tempo which matched the music of the band. The cuts caught the atmosphere of the Café exactly.

Several times Chris Hodson mixed shots from his various takes. One shot on take #1 showing Gregory on the café balcony had a green flare (invisible on the cameraman's black-and-white monitor); so the editor

inserted a few seconds from take #2. But he allowed the sound of #1 to run on because Gregory on #1 was breathing out and would have clashed with the faint sound on #2 of him breathing in. Later Chris Hodson wanted to cut from #2 to #1. He chose a moment when Gregory was moving forward to sit down. It is a safe bet that no one noticed the switch.

This kind of juggling is the mark of good editing. The director must provide the right raw material. Not even the best editor can make an electronic masterpiece out of a sow's ear. But together the editor and director can weld a series of disparate scenes, often shot in the 'wrong' order, into a work of art.

A Perfect Stranger was transmitted on Saturday, 5 January 1974. Seven million households (about 21,420,000 people) watched, making it the eleventh most popular programme of the week.

John Hawkesworth was already at work on the fourth, and last, series. He decided to halt in 1919 because the actors were feeling restless and he believed that the series had had a natural Edwardian life and would not be happy in the Twenties. And he has his eye on a movie: *Upstairs Downstairs*.

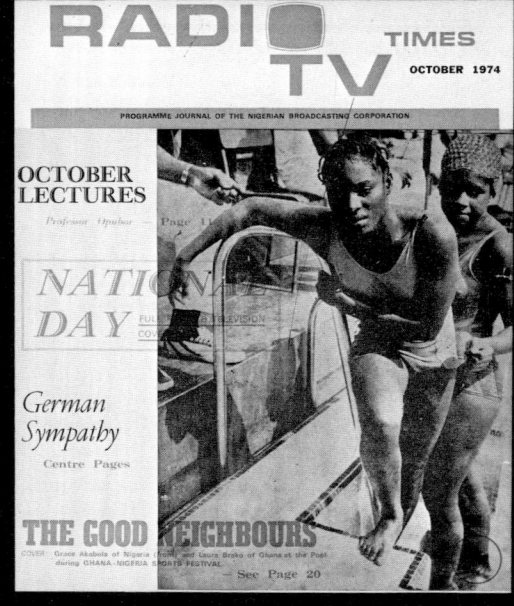
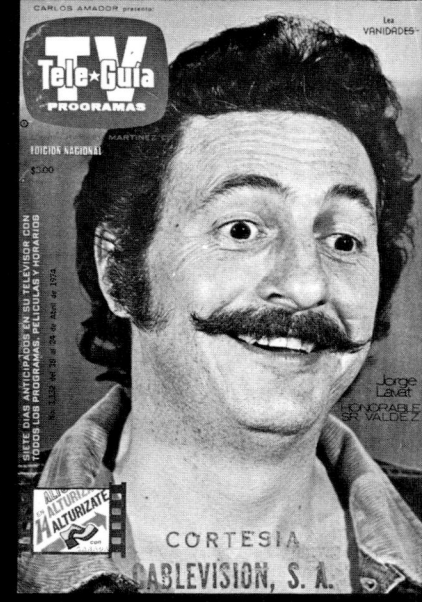

THE TV SYSTEMS AND PROGRAMMES OF THE WORLD

In 1973 ninety-six countries had a regular television service. Each one is different. They range from America's $4,100-million industry to Gibraltar's £40,000 one, from New York's glut of channels to Gibraltar's solitary and part-time one. In some countries like Russia and China the government has complete control over all aspects of broadcasting. In others like America the government has very little control.

Some countries have a sophisticated TV service and a burgeoning tele-generation. But many more countries have only a fledgling service. As we saw, China has only those 600,000 sets, India, even fewer. South Africa will have no public TV until 1976.

But the casual observer might reasonably think that television is roughly the same in every country. From Chicago to Osaka the same familiar TV sets present the same familiar blend of news, entertainment, comedy, drama and late-night discussions. Television does have certain characteristics which support this casual observation. Marshall McLuhan summed them up in his famous phrase: 'The medium is the message'.

Elihu Katz, founding director of Israeli Television, has described the parallel economic pressures which force TV stations to produce the same kind of programmes. The story, he says, is always the same. Take a (mythical) small developing nation. The President starts the ball rolling by announcing grandiose schemes for a national television network to (a) unify the new nation, (b) stimulate cultural activity and (c) spur economic development and education. Six months later the station opens with *I Love Lucy*, *Bonanza* and old Hollywood movies.

Katz suggests that a good independent television service needs three things: adequate money, administrative talent and a long and substantial tradition in the performing arts. The BBC, of course, had all three in abundance. The United States had plenty of the first two and just enough of the third. But most developing countries lack all three. Members of the Commonwealth are lucky since they can draw on the expertise of the BBC; and many of them, such as Nigeria and Ghana for example, have strong traditions of theatre. But most countries, newly independent, are less fortunate. They have nothing for their Opening Night except the Minister's speech and an imported soap opera.

Let us look at the two countries that had sufficient money and administrative talent and two different kinds of traditions in the performing arts and who have developed entirely different broadcasting services. In Britain the BBC is the epitome of public-service broadcasting, and her commercial ITV network has some public-service qualities. The American networks, in contrast, are the epitome of commercial, competitive broadcasting.

THE BBC

PHILIPS clear picture TELEVISION is here — LOOK INTO IT NOW

Philips television receivers for the home embody the results of many years of intensive research and experience with large screen receivers.
Due to the advanced technical features—many of them exclusive to Philips—the new models give a picture of exceptional definition; the details are clear-cut, the picture lighting is brilliant and perfect "viewing" is obtained in ordinary room illumination. Great care has been taken to ensure absolute steadiness of the picture under all conditions.
The Philips range consists of 4 models priced from 32 gns. to 55 gns. and a de luxe large screen receiver at 120 gns.
Philips Clear Picture Television is here! Look into it now! See your dealer to-day!

PHILIPS

PHILIPS LAMPS LTD., CENTURY HOUSE, SHAFTESBURY AVENUE, LONDON, W.C.2.

Type 2407:
A Console model of beautifully balanced proportion and exquisite appearance. Picture size 7½" x 5⅛" with high quality sound accompaniment. 35 Guineas or H.P. terms.

Most people agree that TV is one of the world's most precocious gadgets. But is it important or trivial, beneficial or harmful? The next ten pages show some of the BBC's most famous moments.

Joan Miller, the Switchboard Girl on the weekly *Picture Page*, was one of BBC TV's first personalities.
Here she's taking calls.
Middle: BBC's first television play, 1930.
Below: Chamberlain, in the middle of the picture, faces the TV camera on his return from Germany in 1938.

'It sits there in the corner of the living room relentlessly transmitting its mosaic of life. Image after image, incident after incident, emotion after emotion, juxtaposed with anarchic, confused and irresponsible logic. A man, doused in petrol, sets fire to himself outside the White House. A dentist discovers a gas to destroy mankind. Which is true? Which is false? Does it matter?'
Milton Shulman in *The Ravenous Eye*

What's My Line?, which the BBC bought from America for 25 guineas a show, started in July 1951 with, left to right, Marghanita Laski, Jerry Desmonde, Elizabeth Allen and Gilbert Harding.
Left: The Arsenal team inspect the camera before the first live recording of a football match on September 16, 1937.
Above: the first TV Derby, 1938.

Above: Boys in a Secondary School in Kent watch a schools programme.
Top left: *The Wharf Road Mob*, one of the first dramatised documentaries, showed the lives of teddy boys in London's East End; 1957.
Left: Annette Mills and Muffin the Mule, 1952.
Bottom left: Margot Fonteyn.
Below: *The Grove Family*, a 1950's weekly soap opera about an 'ordinary family'. Christopher Beeny, playing the boy, later starred in *Upstairs Downstairs*.
Right: John Freeman and Bertrand Russell talk to the producer of *Face to Face*, Hugh Burnett.
Bottom right: 'Spaghetti harvesting in the Ticino, Switzerland' was the title of *Panorama*'s April Fool's item on April, 1957. Today's BBC is too pompous to make jokes like this.

A *Panorama* meeting: (from left, clockwise) Rex Moorfoot (later Head of Presentation), Richard Dimbleby, Christopher Chataway (later a Government Minister), John Freeman (later Chairman of LWT), David Wheeler, Woodrow Wyatt (later an MP), Kenneth Lamb (Controller of BBC), Robert Kee and Jeremy Murray-Brown, Christopher Burstall and Margaret Brown, producers.

'For a long time we in Britain thought that the success of our broadcasting lay in the "quality" of the programmes. That was in part true, but in reality the success of the BBC (and ITV, at certain periods) has been that it conscientiously reflects the success of a whole culture in finding some kind of valid relationship with the mass audience, the society at large. That relationship, in Britain as elsewhere, is now under strain and to that extent our "system" is no longer adequate, no matter how great the quality of individual programmes.'
Anthony Smith in *The Shadow in the Cave*

Wilfrid Brambell, above (on the right), and Harry H. Corbett as *Steptoe and Son,* two villainous junk men; 1962.
Left: *Watch with Mother* was an immense success with both mothers and children.
Below left: *Play School*, BBC2's 'progressive' series.
Below right: *The Age of Kings,* a fortnightly history series based on Shakespeare's plays; 1960.

'The villain, the enemy, is the camera. We who are accustomed to working with it know that it is capable of infinite deception, probably the greatest of all deception and yet it is accepted as having some kind of objective truth in it.'
Malcolm Muggeridge, critic and broadcaster

The morning after Z Cars' (top) first episode had been shown, the Chief Constable of Lancashire travelled to London to protest; he said the series attacked the police and had no respect for their job. But 500 episodes later, it remains one of the BBC's most successful series and Charlie Barlow (on the right) gained an (unsuccessful) series called Barlow at Large.
Above: The first TV satire show: That Was The Week That Was with David Frost, Roy Kinnear, Kenneth Cope, Lance Percival and William Rushton. It had only a few performances but an extraordinary and deserved reputation for wit, cheekiness and fun.
Left: Tonight, an early-evening series presented by Cliff Michelmore.

Kenneth Clark's idiosyncratic interpretation of *Civilisation*, right, gave the BBC one of its most successful and proudest moments.
Vote Vote Vote for Nigel Barton, left, Dennis Potter's comedy, had Keith Barron as a political candidate; 1965.
It's a Knockout in Blenheim Palace, middle left (1973): a silly popular game.
The BBC said *Wargame*, bottom left, a film about nuclear attack, was too violent to be shown on TV; cinemas showed it successfully.

Ken Russell is better at making TV than movies; in his *Delius*, left, David Collings talks to Max Adrian; 1968. *Cathy Come Home*, bottom, a Wednesday Play, shocked the country by its emotional story of a family's homelessness; 1966. Johnny Speight's *Till Death Us Do Part*, below, starred Warren Mitchell as a patriotic right-wing bigot. Critics could never decide whether viewers were laughing *at* him or *with* him.

'Communism is Soviet power plus electricity.'
V. I. Lenin, Secretary of Russian Communist Party

'*How can one govern without television?*'
André Malraux, French author and government minister

'*I don't believe in the power of television. No one is influenced by television who doesn't want to be.*'
Eamonn Andrews, broadcaster

Right: Princess Anne and Valerie Singleton on *Blue Peter's* Royal Safari in Africa; 1971.
Below: Monty Python. . . .
Bottom left: *The Space Between Words,* Roger Graef's series of people in different negotiations filmed both their words and the spaces in between; there was no commentary.
Bottom right: John Berger, one of the best TV performers, in his *Ways of Seeing.*

Culloden, a dramatised documentary, bottom left. Dr. Jacob Bronowski, below, another TV 'natural', introducing his brilliant series, *The Ascent of Man*, a humanist interpretation of history.
Open Door, bottom right, gave access to BBC facilities to amateur communicators. Here, Jim Horne introduces the first programme in September, 1973.

The British Broadcasting Corporation enjoys a unique reputation – and most of it is good. In 1936 the BBC (or 'the Beeb' or 'Aunty') used government money, its own talents as a radio broadcaster and the British tradition of theatre to start the world's first regular television service. It has continued to provide a vast range of useful, entertaining and occasionally brilliant programmes and to make and broadcast them to high technical standards.

The BBC is committed financially, artistically and emotionally to public-service broadcasting. Lord Reith, the dour Scottish genius who became the BBC's first Director-General, invented the idea and his successors have stuck to it doggedly. Several other countries, including Canada, Australia and Japan, have paid the BBC the compliment of following in its footsteps.

The BBC's claim to be the best TV in the world is probably true, though its grasp of the title is not very meaningful to itself and not very complimentary to the others. Television stations, and their programmes, are only good and bad in relation to the society they reach. The BBC is a good TV service because its remarkably substantial range of programmes matches British needs much more closely than do the programmes of most other stations match *their* viewers' needs.

China has another good broadcasting system (although severely limited in technical range) because its programmes are suited to the needs of the Chinese people. British viewers would be bored by China's programmes on basic technologies and Chinese viewers would find Britain's intellectual discussions irrelevant and insufferable.

Today, the idea of public-service broadcasting is rather unfashionable. Nobody is sure what it means although a large number of people still respect it as a 'Good Thing'. We can characterize it briefly by two stereotypes: a public-service station produces what it likes to believe the public needs, while a competitive and commercial station produces what it likes to believe the mass audience wants.

In practice, public-service broadcasting is based on three factors: an intimate relationship between the government and the broadcaster signified by the government giving the broadcaster financial support; national coverage; and a serious responsibility to produce programmes that 'inform, educate and entertain'. All governments keep some control over their broadcasters.

A few keep complete control, like Russia, China, most African governments, Spain and Portugal, Greece, most Warsaw Pact countries, Peru and Chile and so on. But most countries allow their broadcasters a degree of freedom.

The BBC is renowned for its peculiar degree of freedom. Lord Reith established the BBC's vital independence during the 1926 General Strike (when the BBC was radio only) and his successors have been anxious to retain it. The result is that the government's ultimate control, in theory and in law, has gone hand in hand with an extreme lack of control in practice, both over the BBC's day-to-day operations and over its long-term policies. This ambiguity has made the BBC strong but vulnerable. The BBC realizes that no one (not even the government) has much control over its policies and programmes, and has reacted in a see-saw fashion. In the 1960s the BBC had a burst of self-confidence and forged a truly national public service. Then it lost its nerve, looked around for advice, found none (because nobody felt authorized to give it) and lapsed into meekness and, worse, paranoia.

The BBC's unique relationship with the British government only works if the BBC is strong and confident. It stands and falls alone.

The government guides this potentially turbulent beast in a number of ways. The most obvious is its control over the level of the licence fee. Everyone in Britain who owns a TV set has to pay an annual licence: £8 for a black-and-white set and £18 for a colour. In 1973 the Government collected £138 million, kept £12 million as rather expensive expenses, and passed £126 million to the BBC for its TV and radio services. The BBC is chronically short of money, and has to accept government guidelines before winning an increase in the licence fee. Other European stations, including those like RAI in Italy and ARD in Germany that accept advertisements, are equally poor. Only the Japanese NHK, whose representatives collect its ¥465 and ¥315 subscription fees door to door, is relatively rich and independent.

These stations' dependence on the public purse is clearly seen in their determination to provide a fully national service. Public-service broadcasters feel guilty about reaching anything less than 95 per cent of the country's homes. The BBC, for instance, covers 99 per cent of British homes whereas ITV covers only 93 per cent. NHK covers 98 per cent of Japanese homes whereas the Japanese commercial stations are content with 92 per cent. ABC has a similar advantage in Australia, and CBC in Canada. The differences may seem small. But the extra investment to reach those last thousands (usually the most distant and isolated communities such as island and mountain villages) is enormous, and indicates a real willingness to provide a national public service.

The third distinguishing mark of a public-service station is its earnest desire to provide a wide range of services. The aim is usually formulated in a trilogy: information, education and entertainment. Actually, the British government instructed both the BBC and ITV to provide 'information, education and entertainment'; it is the range of BBC programmes that demonstrates the station's commitment to public service.

TELEVISION
FOR EVERYBODY

872nd DAY OF TELEVISION
The King and Queen return from Canada. On the screen, thousands of homes watch their triumphant welcome from train to Palace balcony.

INDEPENDENT GROWTH

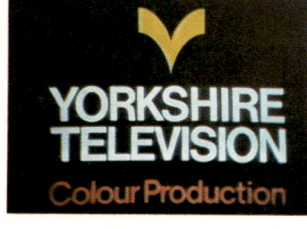

ITV, the UK's commercial network financed by advertising, joined the BBC on September 22, 1955. A grand opening in London's Guildhall was followed by the first ad, for Gibbs SR toothpaste. Within a few months, the bourgeois culture had given way to the commercial hard-sell.

The early, frantic skirmishes of ITV when companies lost and won millions in weeks, lasted a few years. Today, ITV has beaten the BBC in the ratings and is producing as many good programmes. The 1980s may see ITV move into the role of senior broadcaster that the BBC has jealously guarded for so long. Four companies dominate ITV: Granada, London Weekend (LWT), Thames and Yorkshire.

Sir Lew Grade's ATV now concentrates on status – dollars – in North America and elsewhere. The screen logos are shown, right.

Granada's *Sam*, top left, was about growing up in a mining village. The same company's *World in Action* is famous for its investigation of public policy and people, such as John Poulson. Above left: Eamonn Andrews with a *This Is Your Life* book. Above: Hughie Green on one of ITV's first quiz shows, *Double Your Money*. Thames' *World at War*, a million pound 26-part series about World War II, showed that ITV could make major national series as well as the BBC.

Many countries have copied the BBC's maxim of 'information, education and entertainment'. Canada spells it out: 'The National Broadcasting Service should be a balanced service of information, enlightenment and entertainment.' Japan is even more ambitious. The NHK 'shall contribute to the level of civilization by broadcasting rich and good broadcast programmes . . . (and) shall strive to be conducive to the upbringing and popularization of new civilization as well as to the preservation of the past excellent civilization of our country'.

When the Australian government passed its first Television Act in 1963, it was much more modest. Programmes, it said, should be 'adequate and comprehensive' – hardly inspiring. The many commercial stations (the first one opened in Sydney in 1964) share the same weakness.

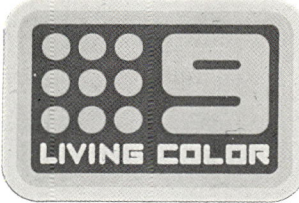

Some of ABC's programmes: *This Day Tonight,* with the leader of the Country Party; *Seven Little Australians,* a Sunday evening serial; and *The Inventors'* panellist Leo Port. Channel 7 has *Homicide* and *The Paul Hogan Show*. Hogan's mate, Strop, is on the left. Ed Singley (here, with Abigail) is one of Channel 9's most popular shows. Channel 10 has a familiar TV police series, *Matlock Police*.

The unambitious level of Australian programmes is revealed in this quotation from the official book, *Television Programme Standards,* published by the Australian Broadcasting Control Board. In most countries, remember, official programme standards aim to raise standards. In Australia, the Board says this: 'It is not intended that the General Programme Standards which follow should prevent the televising in good faith, at appropriate times, and in appropriate circumstances, of artistic or literary works of merit or the serious presentation of moral or social issues. Such programmes are, indeed, to be encouraged, but due warning of their nature should be given, where necessary, both in advance publicity and at the commencement of the programme.' In other words, if you are going to produce a work of art, please warn the viewers first!

A few Australians, fortunately, are aware of the problem. In 1973 the new Labour Government, and Minister of the Media Senator Douglas McClelland, decided to raise programme standards by introducing a points system. Local 'worthy' programmes scored the highest points; imported soap operas scored lowest. Best of all, according to the Government, is an Australian one-off drama. It scores 10 points for a peak-time première, 5 points for an off-peak première, 5 points for a peak-time repeat and 2 points for an off-peak repeat. Next best are arts programmes and 'quality variety', whatever that is. The Government announced that TV stations had to score an average of one point for every hour on the air.

The Australian experience suggests that the concept of public-service broadcasting only works where the country already has a strong tradition of public service, and a belief in the principle of impartial broadcasting. It works in Britain and in countries like Nigeria, Canada and Japan – but not in Australia and America.

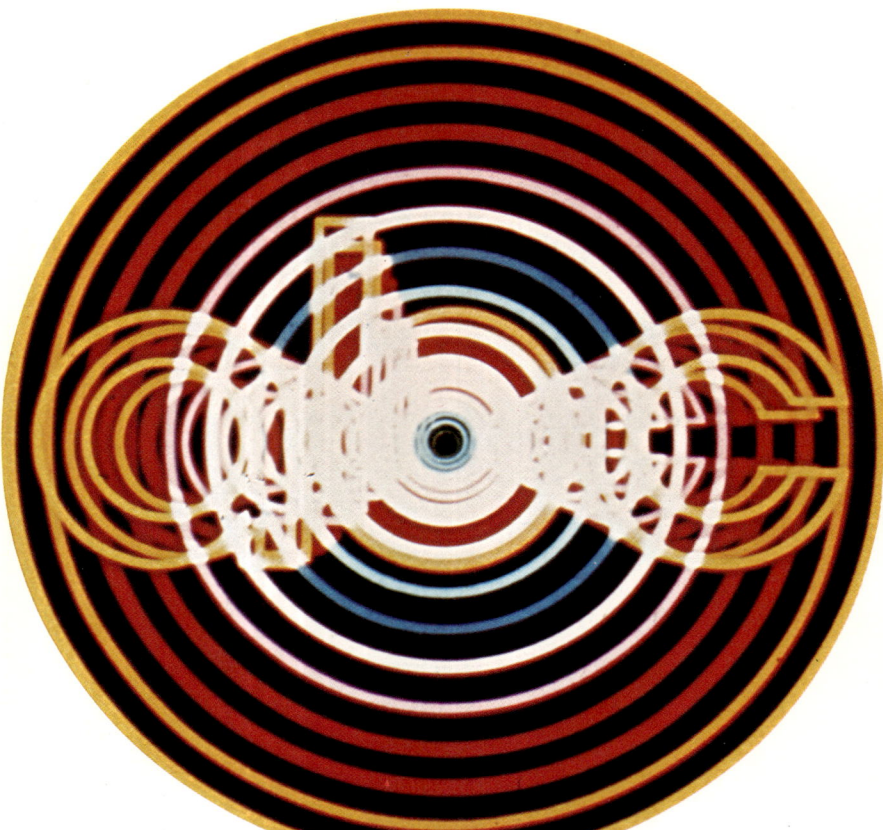

THE AMERICAN NETWORKS

Symbols of the American way of life: ABC's circles, an NBC affiliate's station identification and NBC's peacock.

The transatlantic trade in television programmes, especially drama series, should not disguise the difference between British television, especially the BBC, and the major American networks. Some parts of British broadcasting (Sir Lew Grade's ATV, for example) would fit cosily into the American scene. And some American 'public' stations would feel at home in Britain. But they are exceptions.

American television is big, big business. 20th-Fox's famous sale of its *Poseidon Adventure* (which at $40 million had the biggest gross profit of 1973) catches the fantasy. In 1973 20th-Fox decided to auction the movie between the three networks. Previously, movies had been sold for several TV showings. ABC's record price of $5 million for *Lawrence of Arabia* covered five showings. But 20th-Fox offered *Poseidon* for one showing only. ABC opened the bidding at $2 million. CBS and NBC bid higher, until ABC closed the deal at a staggering record figure of $3·2 million – *for one showing*. Two other events of the same week extend the fantasy. Doris Day

Three memories of US television: *The Lone Ranger,* Senator Joseph McCarthy and a Kraft Theatre play.

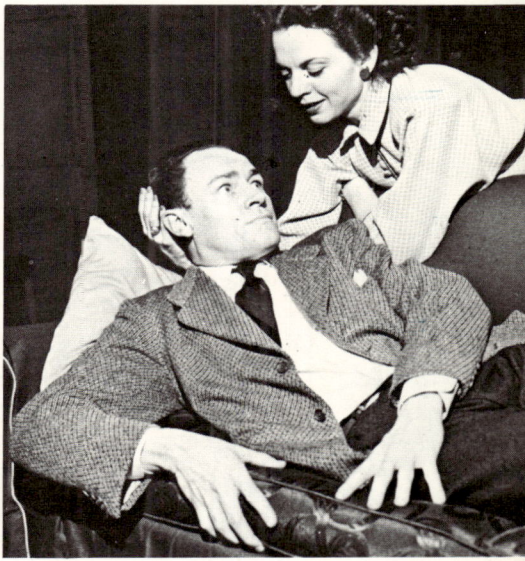

picked up a million dollars for 17 days' work on some General Foods commercials. And, to remind everybody of the industry's deep-seated conservatism, a CBS station turned down the best-selling movie, *The Graduate*.

Two deep-seated American principles governed the creation and early years of American television: free competition and free speech. By the 1950s, the power of free competition had overwhelmed the civil right of free speech. Today, American television dominates American culture. The story is one of competition unconfined.

The government body which nominally controls American broadcasting is the Federal Communications Commission (FCC). The FCC, which has the right to allocate wavelengths and franchises, finds itself unable to fulfil that duty with much success and has even less in its confrontations with the networks over the more important issue of programming. President Nixon showed his disregard for the Commission's independence when he proposed to replace the retiring liberal Commissioner Nicholas Johnson with the conservative James Quello who showed open allegiance to the broadcasting industry.

Britain's contribution to broadcasting is the ideal of public service. America's is the commercial network. The birth of networking (according to the radical and ironically named Network Project) can be fixed at 4 January 1923, when AT&T connected its New York radio station WEAF to its Boston radio station WNAC. By 1924 AT&T had increased its network to 24 stations. Then AT&T and RCA concluded a deal whereby AT&T would retain control of the all-important landlines which made the network possible and RCA would run the stations. In response, the unaffiliated stations formed a rival, United Independent Broadcasters, which later became CBS.

RCA and CBS monopolized American broadcasting for the first ten years, until the FCC forced RCA to hand over one of its networks (the less profitable one) to the newly formed ABC. This trio were the natural inheritors of the new-fangled television. RCA's NBC took the

The *64,000 Dollar Question*; Charles van Doren won $129,000 in 1957 and became a national hero. Phil Silvers as Sgt Bilko and Fess Parker as 1955's Davy Crockett. Richard Nixon lost in 1960 to Jack Kennedy; but learned some valuable lessons for 1973 and the Watergate scandal.

lead and soon owned 52 of the country's 107 television stations. CBS and ABC shared the rest.

What is a network? Surprisingly, NBC, CBS and ABC do not own many stations, nor do they produce many programmes. CBS, NBC and ABC all own the legal maximum of five VHF TV stations and two UHF stations (known as owned-and-operated stations, or o-&-o's). But a company becomes a network only if a number of other TV stations (known as affiliates) promise to take its programmes. The network company delivers the programmes. In return, the affiliate guarantees an audience which the networker can 'sell' to the advertiser. It is a game with high stakes and only three companies have strong hands. CBS has 250 affiliates, NBC has 215 and ABC has 168. A typical affiliate might take around seven hours of networked programmes every day; its peak-time period would be solid network.

Right: That popular rotund private detective: *Cannon*

'It was TV more than anything else that turned the tide.'
President Kennedy after defeating Richard Nixon in 1960

The numbers game works like this. Since 1971 CBS has shown a detective thriller series called *Cannon* starring William Conrad (radio's Matt Dillon) as a fat but fast private detective. In the summer of 1973, when CBS was selling time on *Cannon*'s fourth series, the network salesman went to the advertisers and said: 'Here's a 14th ranked show with a 22·1 rating and a 34 per cent share, and everyone's taking it.'

To translate: CBS was saying that *Cannon*'s 1972/3 series ranked 14th in the Top Thirty and that 22·1 per cent of TV homes watched (on average) giving a total average audience of 14,630,000 homes or 46,816,000 people. At that time (again, on average) 14·6 million homes represented a 24 per cent share of the total audience.

CBS was saying to the advertiser: 'We can deliver 14·3 million homes (they actually said 14·3 homes) and we'll charge you $x a minute.' The actual rates varied, but the average figure was around $60,000 a minute, which works out at $4 for every thousand homes.

CBS sold time to Procter and Gamble, Prudential Insurance, Volkswagen and other major companies, networked the series to its 250 affiliates and made a profit.

The rating figures are the key to the business. Top prime-time shows like *All in the Family, Sanford and Son* and *Hawaii Five-O* got 1972/3 ratings of 33, 27 and 25 and shares around 38 per cent.

Public-service broadcasters are financed by their governments. Commercial broadcasters have to depend on the commercial advertiser. The power of television advertising is immense. One of the earliest success stories is Hazel Bishop's. In 1950 the company sold about $50,000 worth of cosmetics. In 1951 it started to advertise and within two years had sold $4·5 million. The products were unchanged.

But he who pays the piper calls the tune. In 1964 Procter and Gamble, the country's biggest advertiser, refused to advertise on any show that 'gave offense, either directly or by inference, to any organized minority group, lodge or other organizations, institutions, residents of any

97

Grandma in *The Beverly Hillbillies*; crowds in Times Square watching the first US astronaut, Col. John Glenn; *Supermarket Sweep*; Ed Sullivan introduces the Beatles; Johnny Carson with Buddy Hackett, Burt Reynolds and Don Rickles.

State or section of the country or a commercial organization of any sort'.

Chevrolet once censored the phrase 'fording a stream' because it mentioned a competitor. Ford cut a shot of the New York skyline because it showed the Chrysler Building. The American Gas Company cut a Playhouse 90 reference to Nazi extermination camps because it reflected badly on their product.

The advertisers' pressure has forced American television to work a six month year. The TV season starts in mid September, runs flat out until the New Year when the networks replace unsuccessful shows with new ones, then runs for another three months until mid April.

The summer is a jumble of repeats, old movies and pilots for the next season.

American television is a monument to the old film cliché, 'This thing is bigger than both of us'. The 'thing', in this case, is the three network competitive system, and by creating it, man has managed to create a system

'I have confidence in your health but not in your product. I invite you to sit down in front of your television set when your station goes on the air ... and keep your eyes glued to that set till the station signs off. I can assure you that you will observe a vast wasteland.'
Newton Minow, Chairman of the FCC, in a speech to the National Association of Broadcasters, 9 May 1961

Far left: *All in the Family*, the American version of the BBC's *Till Death Us Do Part*, had the rare accolade of being transmitted on BBC1 and getting high ratings. *Sanford and Son*, left, was based on the BBC's *Steptoe and Son*.

James McCord faces the camera — and the Nation; the original *What's My Line?*; *An American Family* (the family lived its troubles on the screen, and finally broke); *Sesame Street,* the hugely successful (commercially and artistically) kids' series.

which is not just 'bigger than both', but imprisons and imposes its disciplines on all three.

There is far too little drama, and far too few documentaries on primetime American television, but the cultured, sophisticated men at the head of the networks – who would personally prefer to watch the dramas and the documentaries – know that to give even one hour away to the opposition, could move their network from 1st to 2nd, with an ensuing loss of hundreds of thousands of dollars in advertising revenue.

The result is that while American television is probably supreme in the areas it has tried and tested – half hour news, variety specials, narrative action series, made-for-television movies – it lacks the diversity, and experimentation possible in a system where not so much is at stake every time the customer decides to switch the dial.

American public stations add their own footnote. These 228 'outsider' stations, loosely amalgamated into a PTV network, finance themselves by viewers' subscriptions, public and private grants and modest sponsorship.

They range from the two prestigious flagships, New York's WNET and Los Angeles' KNET, which produce outstanding documentaries and drama, to more provincial and specialist stations. Few Americans actually watch PTV, perhaps about 2 per cent. But individual stations, and the network, have produced some memorable programmes (including the best-selling *Sesame Street*) and they both provide a basis, a beacon, for public-service broadcasting.

'Well, what can one say? That the networks are trying? They obviously aren't ... I naively expected that the ratio would run three to one in favour of trash. It turned out to be closer to a hundred to one ... I will freely confess that, immediately after my week-long ordeal, I thought that the only way to solve TV's problems was, literally, murder – ie, send in squads of machine gunners and summarily execute every executive at every network and start from scratch.'
Charles Sopkin, who locked himself into his New York flat in April 1967 with five TV sets and watched the entire output from 7 am to 3 am every day for a week.

PROGRAMMES TRAVEL THE WORLD

Americans abroad are sometimes faced with some rather odd questions: 'Is Lorne Greene married?' 'How old is Lucy?' The British abroad face different questions: 'Does John Porter come back from the war?' 'Does Jack divorce Annie?' Each week *Bonanza, Here's Lucy, A Family at War* and *Coronation Street,* which feature these TV heroes, tell their stories to a potential audience of around 500 million people. *Bonanza* alone can reach 300 million. (For apprehensive travellers the answers are: Yes, twice; 63; yes; and never!)

Top: Lorne Greene, hero of *Bonanza*. Across the page, people in Brazil, Poland and Thailand look at a bitchy argument between three working-class women in Britain's *Coronation Street*.

America dominates this international programme market. In 1973, US producers sold almost $90 millions' worth of TV programmes and made-for-TV movies, more than the rest of the world combined. Their profits, however, were modest.

To make one episode of a successful prime-time series like *Bonanza* or *Cannon* costs about $250,000. But even the major potential buyers (Britain, Germany, Canada, France and Japan) will offer only $10,000. Most countries offer less, and TV stations like Malta's MTS and Uganda's UTS would expect to pay around $60.

The problem is twofold. The richer countries, who tend to produce most of their own material, do not need to buy. And the poorer stations cannot afford to. The BBC, for instance, traditionally produces most of its own material. It will happily budget £15,000 or more for an 'inside' documentary, but seldom be prepared to pay more than £3,000 for one produced outside.

Many countries, consequently, practically give away programmes in Asia, Africa and the Middle East in order to keep a foot in the door of these rapidly expanding markets. Some countries go further and deliberately use TV programmes as cultural propaganda – among them, France, Russia and Portugal. ORTF claims to have 'une vocation internationale' with privileged opportunities for 'conveying the activities of metropolitan France to her colonies and around the world'. In 1972 ORTF sold 578 hours of television and gave away over 9,000 hours.

Anyone who hopes to sell – or give away – a television programme faces several tricky obstacles. Several governments, for a start, have imposed strict quotas on foreign programmes to protect their own home TV industry. Australia and Canada, who in the 1960s were deluged with the oldest and worst American shows, have imposed quotas respectively of 50 per cent and 40 per cent. Other quotas range from Peru's unusually high 60 per cent to Britain's low 13 per cent.

Some countries are completely out of bounds. The British government forbids British companies to sell to Rhodesia and ACCT, the British film trade union, is

might have been puzzled, too). Granada had to publish *The American's Guide to Coronation Street* – a glossary of Lancashire expressions.

A totally foreign sound track can be treated in various ways. Some stations leave it on; others completely re-edit the sound and the vision. The first is free and popular (with the purchasing station, anyway). The second is expensive and requires painstaking skill and only the BBC, the German ARD and Japanese NHK are likely to do it. Most buyers compromise by wiping the original sound track and dubbing local actors' voices.

Programme agents must also solve political and cultural barriers. In Europe, for instance, black signifies mourning and white, birth and matrimony. In the Far East the colours are reversed. Humour, too, is definitely not international. Several series have been a roaring success in one country and failed in the next. LWT's *Please Sir!* was shown twice in Britain and twice in the Netherlands, but no American company would give it more than a glance.

All these obstacles conspire against the easy workings of an international programme market, and many stations have turned towards international co-production.

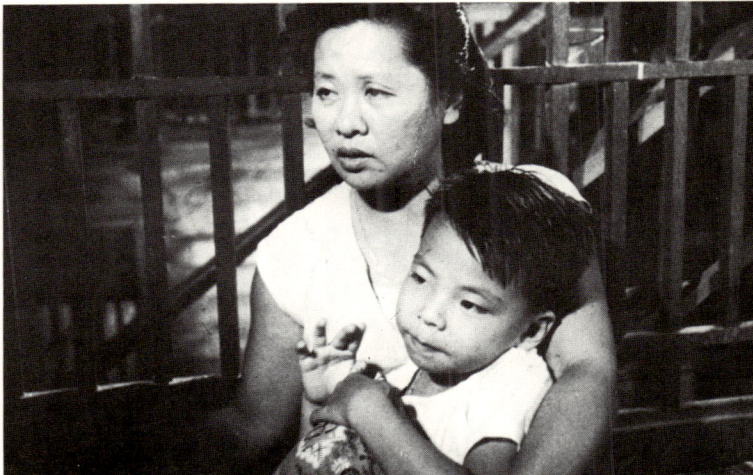

The BBC's *Till Death Us Do Part* has been re-made in Germany and America. It tops the ratings in each country. Here, left, are Else, Alfred, Rita and Michael in the German version.

expected to discourage companies from selling to the imminent South African TV station. But television programmes, like everything else, can be smuggled. Rhodesia regularly shows British TV programmes and South Africa is expected to do the same.

Programme salesmen face several technical obstacles. Programmes on tape, for instance, can be recorded in a variety of different ways. If an American producer sells a programme to Britain he has to convert the American standard tape (525 line, NTSC colour, 60 hz) to the British standard (625 line, PAL colour, 50 hz).

Foreign sound tracks are tricky for everyone. It is not surprising that four of the six major programme markets speak the same language. More or less, anyway. When Britain's Granada sold *Coronation Street* to New York's WNET they discovered that even the station staff could not understand some of the Lancashire colloquialisms: Pandas, chip butties, nowt and the slate (some Britons

The basic difference between the two is that co-production guarantees the producer a sum of money before production, while a sales market offers him only the chance of a smaller sum after it. The European stations have been most eager to co-produce since they are most short of money. The BBC has co-produced with several German stations, its American distributor *Time-Life*, British Petroleum, American public stations, several Commonwealth stations and Japan. Sir Lew Grade, the energetic showman who heads ATV, has used co-productions to break into the lucrative American market. In 1973, for instance, he and RAI co-produced a mammoth £1·5-million series *The Law-Giver* with Burt Lancaster as Moses and sold it, before shooting a foot of film, to the American CBS.

ALTERNATIVES AND THE FUTURE

Every nation has developed its own brand of broadcasting – usually a mixture of public-service and commercial. Some countries add education. Japan has two 'public-service' channels and one is exclusively educational. Israel would like to have the same; meanwhile, it splits the solitary IBA channel between education and general programmes.

African countries are most devoted to educational television. In the early 1960s both Niger and the Ivory Coast carried out substantial experiments. They hoped to cure their appalling illiteracy problem (Niger's illiteracy rate is 99 per cent) and, within the limits of the experiment, they succeeded. The Ivory Coast has recently signed an ambitious 10-year, £200-million project with UNESCO and the World Bank.

The Ghanaian television service is firmly educational. The National Redemption Council ensures that GTV broadcasts several hours of schools TV every day and that all peak-time programmes convey a social message. Zanzibar spoke for these countries when she publicly announced her dislike of 'America's desperate Westerns'. Both Zanzibar and Ghana have managed to keep their imports of all foreign programmes below 14 per cent.

Other countries have added *access* – usually after an admiring glance at Dutch broadcasting (which is not, however, without its faults). The Dutch system is unique, an extraordinary fusion of public-spirited and commercial broadcasting. The kingpin of the system is the Netherlands Broadcasting Foundation, which takes one third of the airtime for its own news, current affairs, sports and education, and allocates the remaining two thirds to seven public groups, providing them with offices and studios. The four largest 'A' groups, with more than 400,000 membership out of a population of 13 million, qualify for eight hours every week. They are the general AVRO, the socialist VARA, the Protestant NRCV and the Roman Catholic KRO. At present, there are no 'B' groups, but there are three 'C' groups with membership between 100,000 and 250,000 which qualify for 2½ hours weekly: the liberal VPRO, the conservative TROS and the Evangelical EO.

The Dutch thus reflect their political and religious groupings in their broadcasting much more deliberately and specifically than anyone else. During the international oil shortage of 1973/4, for example, the Dutch were able to present seven completely different discussions, one of which, a VPRO late-night show, was the

worldwide television

Country	Population 000,000s	No of TV sets 000,000s	Colour System	Average Price 30 mins episode $	Average Price Feature Film $
Abu Dhabi	0.050	0.015	—	30	70
Afars and Issas	0.008	0.003	—	20	80
Alaska	0.3	0.003	—	25	300
Albania	2.1	0.003	—	40	400
Algeria	13.3	0.150	—	100	50
Argentina	23.3	3.40	—	700	3,000
Australia	12.7	3.00	PAL	3,000	25,000
Austria	7.3	1.63	PAL	400	1,600
Barbados	0.25	0.025	NTSC	45	700
Belgium	9.6	2.95	PAL	400	1,600
Bolivia	4.8	0.011	—	30	50
Bermuda	0.052	0.018	NTSC	30	140
Brazil	93.0	6.58	—	1,600	6,000
Bulgaria	8.4	1.24	Secam	70	50
Canada	21.5	7.60	NTSC	3,200	10,000
CBC (English)					
CBC (French)	21.5	7.60	NTSC	2,750	5,000
CTV	21.5	7.60	NTSC	1,750	7,500
Canary Islands	1.2	0.20	—	20	100
Chile	9.56	0.50	—	70	375
China	723.0	0.60	—	30	50
Columbia	20.4	0.60	—	200	850
Costa Rica	1.69	0.12	—	40	175
Cuba	8.55	0.36	—	30	50
Cyprus	0.63	0.06	—	30	125
Czechoslovakia	14.4	3.10	Secam	200	1,250
Denmark	4.9	1.50	PAL	225	1,100
Dominica	4.3	0.15	—	55	240
Ecuador	5.9	0.15	—	55	175
Egypt	34.0	0.57	—	165	600
El Salvador	3.3	0.10	—	35	160
Ethiopia	23.6	0.008	—	30	100
Finland	4.7	1.18	PAL	300	1,100
France	51.0	12.40	Secam	2,900	7,500
Gabon	0.47	0.005	—	30	100
West Germany	61.5	17.8	PAL	3,500	16,000
East Germany	17.0	4.5	Secam	375	1,600
Ghana	8.5	0.02	—	40	100
Gibraltar	0.026	0.006	—	30	100
Greece	8.7	0.270	—	130	500
Guadeloupe	0.312	0.009	—	30	80
Guam	0.058	0.042	NTSC	40	100
Guatemala	4.8	0.082	—	50	170
Haiti	4.6	0.012	—	25	90
Hawaii	0.75	0.350	—	300	900
Honduras	2.5	0.045	—	30	100
Hong Kong	4.1	0.300	—	75	300
Hungary	10.3	2.100	Secam	130	500
Iceland	0.203	0.044	—	30	100
India	546.0	0.021	—	30	50
Indonesia	122.0	0.236	—	75	250
Iran	28.0	0.260	—	110	420
Iraq	9.5	0.350	—	115	225
Ireland	3.0	0.540	PAL	130	300
Israel	3.0	0.540	PAL	150	500
Italy	53.3	10.831	PAL	750	7,000
Ivory Coast	4.2	0.075	—	40	100
Jamaica	1.86	0.084	—	35	100
Japan	104.6	23.100	NTSC	3,500	25,000
Jordan	2.25	0.060	—	40	100

first to reveal Shell's private rationing of oil deliveries.

The Dutch system has the advantage of independence and multiple access but it lacks the guts and skills of professional broadcasting. The bulk of afternoon and peak-time programmes are American and British imports (the Netherlands, after all, is too small to support its own movie or TV industry). AVRO shows *Peyton Place*, NRCV *Softly Softly*, VARA *Coronation Street* and KRO *Bonanza*. And *Bonanza* is hardly famous for its Catholic morality.

The worldwide trend is towards greater decentralization and commercialism. New Zealand is typical. In the late 1960s New Zealanders were getting frustrated and irritated by their NZBC (a sort of BBC) which, it was claimed, was proving insensitive to the country's changing needs. They appointed an international commission that split the monolithic NZBC into four separate corporations: one for the existing TV network, one for the projected second network, one for the radio network and one, the NZ Broadcasting Authority, for news and common services. It seems cumbersome, but it might achieve the government's aims: 'to decentralize control and introduce competitive enterprise'.

New Zealand was unusual in the extent and thoroughness of its reforms. Once started, television is hard to stop; and television systems harder still. The US networks, the BBC and NHK, Germany's federal ARD – these powerful institutions will not undergo change willingly. French broadcasters tried to reform ORTF's monopoly for years. The results were appalling. In the 1973 ORTF handbook Arthur Comte, the government's latest appointment to the Director-General's hot seat, asked: 'Radio et Television, qu'est-ce?' He was sacked before he could find the answer. His successor Marceau Long has a different slogan: 'I am the last chance for the monopoly.' The French have rallied, and the monopoly was doomed. ORTF officially closed down on January 1, 1975. Its successors now face the old problems. The Italian RAI and the Israeli IBA are undergoing equal traumas; almost everyone wants change but nobody knows how to achieve it.

Peru solved the problem in the most dramatic fashion – by nationalizing all the TV companies. For years, the country's 19 stations had been churning out repetitive song-and-dance *novelas* and American imports (the merit of a *novela* is that a nifty director could make one before lunch and two after it). After a spirited confrontation between the Minister and the three families who ran most of the companies, the Government nationalized all stations, set up worker communities and declared that every station must broadcast general and educational programmes in the national interest.

But most countries move more slowly: adding a channel here, allowing a few more minutes of advertising there, and so on. Certainly, the trends towards educational TV, access, greater independence and more commercialism will be strongly filtered and affected by each country's local conditions.

Country						Country					
Kenya	10·8	0·034	—	30	50	Reunion	0·43	0·023	—	30	80
Cambodia	7·0	0·025	—	30	100	Rhodesia	5·310	0·051	—	30	50
Korea	31·0	0·100	—	30	100	Romania	20·0	1·843	—	175	150
Kuwait	0·733	0·125	—	75	300	St Pierre &					
Lebanon	2·65	0·320	Secam	55	225	Miquelon	0·005	0·001	—	30	50
Leeward Islands	0·005	0·001	—	180	200	Sabah	0·656	0·002	—	30	50
Liberia	1·13	0·008	—	30	50	Samoa	0·027	0·003	—	30	50
Libya	1·87	0·002	—	20	50	Saudi Arabia	0·720	0·122	—	55	300
Luxembourg	0·34	0·081	Secam	180	200	Senegal	3·8	0·02	—	30	40
Madeira	0·270	0·004	—	30	50	Sierra Leone	2·50	0·005	—	30	50
Malagasy	6·60	0·005	—	20	50	Singapore	2·03	0·193	—	55	190
Malaysia	1·58	0·260	—	50	180	South Africa	21·3		(in 1976)		
Malta	0·322	0·066	—	28	50	Spain	33·7	4·4	PAL	500	3,000
Martinique	0·350	0·011	—	30	50	Sudan	15·5	0·06	—	30	50
Mauritius	0·800	0·023	—	40	80	Sweden	8·0	2·67	PAL	450	1,300
Mexico	48·4	4·000	NTSC	775	1,200	Switzerland	6·27	1·49	PAL	160	1,300
Monaco	0·023	0·016	—	130	150	Syria	6·30	0·135	—	60	105
Mongolia	1·27	0·002	—	30	50	Tahiti	0·061	0·012	—	30	50
Morocco	15·0	0·225	—	50	100	Taiwan	14·8	1·000	NTSC	55	200
Mozambique	7·36	0·005	—	30	60	Thailand	34·8	0·648	PAL	140	650
Netherlands	13·0	3·320	PAL	560	1,850	Trinidad and					
Netherland						Tobago	1·044	0·070	—	30	80
Antilles	0·216	0·033	—	30	100	Tunisia	4·53	0·080	—	30	80
New Caledonia	0·100	0·011	—	30	50	Turkey	35·6	0·015	—	30	50
New Zealand	2·86	0·708	PAL	300	800	Uganda	9·7	0·015	—	30	50
Nicaragua	1·80	0·060	—	30	175	United Kingdom	55·4	19·5	PAL	4,000	25,000
Nigeria	66·17	0·075	—	30	100	USA	206·8	93·0	NTSC	20,000	100,000
Norway	3·87	0·900	PAL	175	375	USSR	241·7	40·0	—	30	60
Pakistan	55·0	0·120	—	50	140	Upper Volta	5·43	0·004	—	30	60
Panama	1·41	0·158	—	50	150	Venezuela	10·7	0·980	NTSC	500	3,000
Paraguay	2·36	0·051	—	40	100	Vietnam (South)	17·8	0·500	—	100	300
Peru	13·17	0·410	—	120	750	Virgin Islands	0·070	0·028	—	30	60
Philippines	37·00	0·430	NTSC	200	700	Yemen Arab					
Poland	32·59	4·250	Secam	175	500	Republic	5·72	0·025	—	30	60
Portugal	8·98	0·524	—	175	500	Yugoslavia	21·5	2·240	—	80	300
Puerto Rico	2·71	0·600	NTSC	500	3,500	Zaire	17·1	0·005	—		
Qatar	0·130	0·027	—	30	80	Zambia	4·06	0·020	—	50	100

TELEVISION GOES LOCAL

In Toronto there is a rather special TV station. It serves two blocks of flats. The studio is in the basement of one of the blocks and doubles as a coffee lounge. Every few hours somebody comes in, prepares a news and information bulletin ('The next meeting of the Theatre Group has been postponed till 7 pm . . . Mrs Freeman in 14 has lost a blue parcel of clothes . . . Berretts has a special delivery of blankets at $5·50') and transmits it on the blocks' special cable into every flat. When the bulletin is finished he (or more likely she) swivels the camera so that it points out of the window. People in the flats can then see if their children are OK and if the delivery man has come. In the evening, different groups present local programmes.

Toronto's TelApart cable TV service is local television. The phrase 'local television' indicates a TV system which shows TV material to small local populations (usually 50,000 or fewer people).

Chapter 1 dealt with satellites and their effects – their creation, almost, of international television. This chapter deals with two other technological innovations which have practically created local television: portapaks and cable TV.

The practitioners of local television have used a multitude of words to capture its flavour: community television, barefoot television, access television, participation – even Do-It-Yourself television. Local community television is not just a small-scale, junior version of national, peak-time TV. It is something totally different, with enormous implications for the whole future of television – the future, perhaps, of communications.

The titles of the basic handbooks on this New Television are revealing: *Guerrilla Television* and *Community Access Video*. And the basic magazine is called *Radical Software*.

Here's a comment from *Radical Software* called 'Public Access: The Second Coming of Television':

In some parts of New York City today a dial twister with cable television could be looking at some pretty unusual programmes. Often unannounced, and without titles, these programmes pop on to the screen to run for half-an-hour or an hour sometimes breaking up into stripes, occasionally vanishing into snow, leaving the viewer with only the sound to help unravel the mystery of what the programme is, and who is doing it. But for some people these programmes on the new Public Access cable channels in Manhattan are charged with an excitement unequalled by anything television has ever done, their very presence a crazy miracle, a chance to change the course of the nation's most promising and least fulfilled mass communications medium.

The New Television is a potent mixture of extravagant ambitions but unwieldy, insufficient resources. The ambitions are certainly pitched high. As one writer has said: 'We're trying to change society and it might take a little time.' *Radical Software* details the inadequate resources in the same article:

The Sterling-Manhattan cable system has only one half-inch playback deck which is kept on an old card table in the corner of the studio. Moreover, they have no switcher so that even if you bring up your own deck there's still an interval between tapes when the engineer patches from one to the other. And it's not uncommon for the engineer to miss the end of a tape because he's on his coffee break or chatting with someone in the other room. The result is intolerable dead time on the screen.

It sounds a far cry from the precise and lavish production of *Bonanza* and *I Love Lucy*, and it is, and it would provide viewers who are bored with Lorne Greene and Lucy a refreshing alternative.

The roots of the New Television lie in (i) the invention of cheap videotape recorders and (ii) the simultaneous exploitation of cable television. Let us start by looking at videotape.

107

Many local community groups have used portapaks to explore local issues. The results are often personal and unpredictable.

Portapak or DIY TV

The first television programmes, in the 1930s, were either filmed or transmitted live. The choice was really no choice at all. Film was expensive and cumbersome. So most television was live. Actors dashed behind the cameras to get from one set to another; singers had to sing all their songs and comics had to remember all their jokes without a break; and advertisers had to go in front of the live camera, say their piece, and get off. It was great fun, chaotic and infuriating.

America was doubly inconvenienced with several different time zones. The New York television stations wanted to record a programme for the New York peak time and then show it across the continent, one, two and three hours later. They could not do it.

A small company called Ampex, significantly situated on the far West Coast, solved the problem in 1954 by inventing videotape. Videotape works exactly like audio-tape but more so. It records both sounds *and* pictures. A videotape recorder (VTR), like an ordinary tape recorder, records electrical impulses on magnetic tape.

The 1¼ cm. (½ in.) tape of the Sony Portapak (camera and videotape recorder) may be transferred to 2½ or 5 cm. (1 or 2 in.) for transmission. Below, Bristol Channel in the UK interviews a local councillor.

The tape can be played back immediately – and many times. Videotape quickly began to revolutionize TV production. Today the majority of television programmes are recorded on videotape (although film dominates in peak time because of the large proportion of movies). Tape is cheaper, safer and quicker.

The next major breakthrough was Sony's introduction of the first lightweight, portable and cheap videotape recorder and camera in 1967: the Port-a-Pak, nowadays called portapak.

The portapak has two parts: a camera and a VTR. The camera weighs 4 lb and has a built-in TV monitor for a viewfinder. The VTR weighs 12 lb and has its own microphone and batteries. The whole bag of tricks costs around £700 (although discount shops in America, Britain and Japan sell them for nearer £600). The tape itself can take some 60 different recordings and about 2,000 playbacks, and costs about £7 for 30 minutes (film stock, by comparison, costs nearer £40 without processing).

A portapak is as simple to operate as an ordinary tape recorder. *Community Access Video* gives this advice: 'The half-inch video systems are so simple in method of set-up and operation that, in a couple of hours, we've had 7th grade kids using the system themselves. So don't be put off by the Wizard of Oz aura of television and don't fear screwing-up.' It really is simple. You strap the recorder on your back, pick up the camera, press two buttons and start making TV.

Portapaks are as versatile as a home movie outfit. Do you remember the odd and exhilarating sensation of seeing yourself, for the first time, in a mirror or a photograph? And for the first time seeing your profile; discovering, in fact, that you *had* a profile? And the thrill of seeing yourself in a film? Perhaps on television? Each time extended your awareness of what you look like – even of who you are. Video's instant playback is the next step. You can see yourself being camera-shy, and then smiling, as you look at the camera and smile. The New Television calls this video-as-process.

Seeing yourself seeing yourself, so to speak, can be unnerving. Africans of the nineteenth century felt a sharp sense of fear and loss when they saw themselves represented in the white explorers' fuzzy photographs. People have felt a sharp sense of intimidation when seeing themselves on a television screen. Nobody knows the effects of this kind of self-perception.

Video-as-process depends on *feedback*. Feedback is a woman looking in a hand compact and adding more mascara (or taking it off); a comedian practising his jokes in front of a full-length mirror; a chat-show presenter looking at a TV monitor and shifting his shoulders to a more dignified position. Feedback is the information that causes a person to change his behaviour.

Video's instantaneous playback can be used to re-affirm a desired image or to reveal the possibility of new images. Salesmen, for instance, use video to improve their sales pitch and ambitious executives use it to improve their speechmaking. But drama teachers use video to demonstrate new opportunities for new movements, psychotherapists use video to increase their patients' self-awareness, and so on.

The over-crowded air... cable TV arrives

The main activity of the New Television is more familiar: making television programmes. Not so much video-as-process as video-as-product.

America's 1972 party conventions showed this New Television in vigorous action. The three main networks traditionally give both the Democratic and Republican conventions blanket coverage when they are staged every four years. In 1972 they spent the fantastic sum of $22 million. CBS even spent $100,000 on a special glass box for Walter Cronkite, their lead commentator.

Ant Farm and Raindance, two of America's most radical video groups, decided to produce a sort of 'home movie' of the conventions. They wanted to be more intimate and more revealing than the networks. They formed a fantasy project called Top Value Television (or TVTV), raised $12,000, hired a house in Miami, organized ten teams with portapaks, and started to record. The teams' instructions were informal but direct: 'When you get to a spot it's up to you to determine if your energy is being well spent. If you think you need more help then call the house and we'll provide what's available.'

The major networks were concentrating on the official and routine events frontstage. TVTV went backstage and offstage for the party meetings, the strategy discussions, the gossip, the rehearsals, the successes and the mistakes. They talked to politicians who thought the convention was marvellous and they talked to Miami residents who wished the politicians would take their convention 'someplace else'. They talked to Julie and Tricia Nixon, and to Walter Cronkite in his glass box.

Cronkite, honest as ever, replied to their criticisms of the networks' own coverage by saying: 'Sure, if we had only television, it would be disastrous.' They recorded the speeches, the confusion and hassles, the nonsense and the brouhaha and they recorded themselves recording it. They even filmed their own reporter, bearded Skip Blumberg, playing the harmonica on an almost empty convention floor while he waited for something to happen.

The first tape, on the Democratic Convention, was called The World's Largest Television Studio after the vast, cavernous Convention Hall. TVTV sold it to a Chicago UHF station and some cable systems, raised another $8,500 and went back to tape the Republican Convention. The second tape, Four More Years, was shown on the Group W network, several off-air stations and several cable systems including the country's largest in Manhattan.

The network professionals were overwhelmed. They were already disappointed with their own coverage. One network reporter described his own network's coverage on the TVTV tape as 'a packaged plastic kind of meeting with no spontaneity. I'm put off by the way we're concentrating on the platform'.

A CBS man admitted: 'Our network spent more on coffee than those kids did to cover both Conventions, and they did a better job.'

Hundreds of different groups from TVTV to the Inter-Action community arts group in London have realized that the portapak's lightness, flexibility and low cost enables ordinary people to produce programmes that the television corporations, with their sophisticated, cumbersome and expensive equipment seem to have lost the ability – and perhaps the will – to make.

Sending TV signals through the air is cheap but inefficient. In 1945 the International Telecommunications Union (ITU), which allocates the world's airwaves, gave the American FCC 83 television channels: 13 VHF channels and 70 UHF channels. For a variety of reasons, most of them bad, the FCC decided to restrict American TV stations to the 13 VHF channels. The FCC, actually, was restricting stations to six or seven channels, since signals in adjacent channels interfere with each other and the stations could not use every channel. In the 1950s the VHF channels began to fill up and the FCC realized its mistake, but it was too late.

The ITU also gave Britain 13 VHF channels (and 44 UHF channels) and the Government, again for a variety of controversial reasons, decided to use them for broadcasting one identical national service (adding a second in 1955 and a third in 1962). Britain currently has one spare UHF channel and will have two spare VHF channels in the late 1970s. But no more. The outlook for local community TV, then, could be grim. The airwaves over America, Britain, Japan and Germany are fully booked.

The solution could be cable television. Cable television simply means that the TV signals do not travel through the air and arrive at an aerial, but are sent through an underground cable to arrive at a set-side terminal.

A cable system consists of a master antenna and a network of underground co-axial or twin-pair cables. The TV signal arrives at the antenna (the head end) and travels along the cable to individual sets. The cable operator can also inject his own TV signals at the head end and send them along the cable. The cable, then, can carry not only the local station's television programmes but locally originated programmes.

The star of cable television is the cable itself. A co-axial cable is misleadingly thin and bendy. It can easily carry 20 or 40 or more television channels as well as several radio programmes and telephone calls.

111

A cable television system develops in three distinct stages. The same phrase, 'cable TV', is used for each:
1 *CATV* (community antenna television) the retransmission of previously broadcast television programmes.
2 *Local Origination* the local origination or production of additional television programmes.
3 *Two-Way Cable* a cable which allows both the station operator *and the subscriber* to originate, produce, TV signals.

This chapter concentrates on (2) Local Origination, leaving the two-way cable to the next.

Several US towns have made rival claims to be the inventor of CATV. In Lansford, Pennsylvania, the story goes that the town's TV salesman, Robert J Tarlton, was having great difficulty in selling his sets because local reception was so bad. In early 1949, Tarlton had a bright idea: to build his customers' antennae on a nearby hill top. In the autumn, he produced his invention: all his customers should share one big antenna. He borrowed some money, formed the Panther Valley Television Company – and never looked back. Customers happily paid $125 for installation and $3 rent. Soon everyone was doing it, especially smaller towns in rocky areas, which often lacked their own television stations.

The first cable systems were replicas of Mr Tarlton's. They picked up local TV signals and retransmitted them along the cable. But in the late 1960s cable operators began to look more closely at the vast – and still unused – capacity of cable for more channels.

A few cable operators started to make their own programmes. The first programmes, actually, hardly deserved the name. Enterprising operators merely bought a black-and-white camera and pointed it at the nearest wall clock or a barometer or temperature gauge, or an AP ticker-tape machine. It was easy, it was cheap and it attracted a few more subscribers.

Gradually, the operators got more ambitious. They began to regard themselves as broadcasters. They stopped talking about CATV head ends and started talking about TV stations. The control room became a studio. The manager became a programme controller. His office staff became a production team.

The Sloan Report, published in 1971, gave these cable enthusiasts a public manifesto. It promised a vision of a 'wired nation' with a comprehensive cable network, owned by the community, connecting home and home, office and office. The news of 3,000 humble head ends turning themselves, without any government say-so, into self-confident and ambitious TV stations affronted both the professional pride and (much more important) the financial plans of the entire American broadcast industry.

The debate soon boiled down into two central issues. First, who should own the cable? Should it be the big media corporations, who want to capture cable as they have already captured television, radio and publishing? Or a local democratic association such as a public authority or a community group? Surely, people said, local communities should control their own communication channels? Second, how local is local? Should cable systems be permitted to import distant signals (say, from stations 200 miles away)? Should cable systems be permitted to link up and form a fourth network – a cable network?

In America, the debate is confused by the reluctance of the government agency, the FCC, to use its regulatory powers. The FCC tends to support the cablecasters (although the Commission's allegiance weakened after 1974 with the departure of the strongest pro-cable Commissioners, Chairman Dean Burch and Nicholas Johnson), but the broadcast industry retains control.

The FCC, however, is the traditional authority and it has supported the cablecaster's right to import distant signals and to produce his own programmes. Dean Burch has made his own preferences very clear: 'If cable television amounts to no more than a new way to move TV signals around, then we in the US would have no compelling interest in its evolution. We are interested in its literally explosive potential for new, diverse and valuable services. For us, it is cable's non-broadcast capabilities that constitute its real promise.'

Enthusiasts of the New Television agree. They pin their hopes on cable's vast capacity for 20, 40 or more channels. Most people expect the major networks, the FCC notwithstanding, to gain control of the bulk of the new cable systems. But surely, they argue, not even an American network can manage to fill so many tens of channels with programmes – however energetically they scrape the barrel.

But the FCC, quite rightly, is not taking any chances. From 1972, every US cable station had to provide at least twenty channels with (i) an equal number of broadcast and non-broadcast channels and (ii) five 'access' channels including one free channel on a first-come, first-served basis.

In 1972, America had over 3,000 CATV stations serving 6·5 million subscribers (about 10 per cent of TV homes) in 5,500 different communities. Most of the systems, like the original one in Lansford, were small and rural, but an increasing number were situated in the major cities.

America and Canada (where almost 30 per cent of TV homes subscribe to a system) have encouraged cable for many years, but Europe and Japan, the only other cable regions, have been more hesitant. Most of Britain's two million subscribers are offered only retransmitted programmes. In 1972 the government half-heartedly gave licences for local origination to five groups: the two main cable companies (Rediffusion and British Relay), one Canadian company and an association of local TV traders. The five stations in Bristol, Swindon, Sheffield, Greenwich and Wellingborough started cablecasting about one hour of local programmes a day. Initial results have been mixed, and Bristol and Greenwich closed after two years.

The French government, like the British, is keen to retain its control over broadcasting and has been chary of handing over 'the right to communicate' to newcomers. But a small experiment was authorized in Grenoble in 1972.

In the Netherlands the cablecasters were more vigorous and the government more generous. Several cable stations started unofficially to produce original programmes in 1971; then the government closed them down on Christmas Eve. But after a year of debate and compromise it authorized six experimental stations to produce local programmes for two years, and gave them 450,000 guilders to do so.

Italy started cable with an explosion. Two little portapaks actually brought down the government. It happened like this. The Italian government holds a tight control over RAI, the TV and radio service, and is jealous of any competition. It allows wired radio, *la filodiffusione*, and the unique daily news service, *il giornale radio-telefonico*, but it has resisted any attempt to start cable television.

In 1972 RAI's twenty-year-old charter expired. The government promptly extended it for one year while it decided what to do. Did Italy need another channel? Did Italy *want* another channel? Should RAI adopt PAL or Secam colour (a question overloaded with political significance)? Above everything, one big question: should the RAI monopoly be ended? Nobody could decide what to do. Except Beppo Sacchi. That winter, he started a guerrilla cable service in Biella, thirty miles in the hills north of Milan. He bought two portapacks and strung the cables from telephone wires. During the week, he cablecast gossip scandals, and local information. At weekends, he put TV monitors in the main square to catch shoppers, pedestrians, tourists, anyone.

The government was horrified. RAI protested that TeleBiella was interfering with its own transmissions (an unlikely and unproven accusation). Signor Gioia, the Minister of Posts and Telecommunications, decided to sneak through parliament a decree giving the state-owned STET a monopoly over cable. He got it through without a debate and announced it as law. There was uproar. TeleBiella challenged the decree in the courts. The courts declared the decree to be illegal and more uproar ensued. The country was disgusted at the Minister's underhand tactics. He even seemed incapable of doing the job for which he was elected: formulating a law. The government realized its fate and resigned.

The future

The battle between the broadcasters and the cablecasters is one of the most important confrontations of the 1970s. Americans fired the first volleys but the war is being fought in Canada, Britain, France, the Netherlands, Italy, Belgium, Germany and Japan.

The existing broadcasting industries want to commandeer cable for their traditional consensus patterns of programming. The New Television enthusiasts want to exploit cable as an instrument of choice – with new and 'alternative' programmes. The two groups can co-exist. But only the watchful eye of a strong and independent public authority can ensure that they co-exist peacefully.

The New Television is cheap and populist. It gives an opportunity to make television, and distribute it, to numerous groups who have been excluded from the existing broadcasting elites. It provides an electronic soapbox. A local TV station can afford to be orientated to its local minorities such as the badly housed or immigrants, or pensioners. A national station cannot afford to be so exclusive. It is this combination of cheapness and radical politics that gives the New Television its unique value: a combination of cheapness and cheek.

One of the best programmes of the New Television is *King Heroin*, a locally originated programme that New York's TelePrompter station showed in late 1970. *King Heroin* was written and performed by an amateur East Harlem theatre group. Jack Gould, the respected *New York Times* TV critic, wrote this:

> This week marks a chapter in the evolution of communications. Electronics can and will expand the audience for truly community theatre. . . . It demonstrates anew that slick settings and fancy camera work are no substitute for authority, integrity and a willingness to experiment. King Heroin stands as one form of tomorrow's TV (and shows) how much can be accomplished on a modest scale given the will and the conviction.

King Heroin.

TV TOMORROW

The 1970s are reminding us of television's original, proper definition: any image reproduced at a distance. People are starting to make their own television, which would have been unthinkable ten years ago, and to show it to their friends or on a local cable system. Soon, the cable will be two-way and people will be able to use television (images-at-a-distance) to order anything from groceries to a newspaper – or even an old-style programme.

TWO-WAY CABLE

The first co-axial cable surpassed off-air channels as much as the first superhighway surpassed a winding farm track. The trouble was that these first superhighways were one-way. All the traffic had to go in the same direction: from the cable station to the subscriber's set.

The problem, luckily, has two simple solutions. We can lay a second cable alongside the first and send messages station-to-set along the first and set-to-station along the second. Or we can use different frequencies inside the one cable. (Both solutions, of course, require a simple terminal at the subscriber's end.)

The dividing line between one-way and two-way cable is in fact often blurred. Two-way cable ranges from (a) the simplest systems with one-way audio-and-video and a return channel with an on-off bleeper to (b) the capacity to send and return audio and video in equal strength.

Bell Telephone introduced a fully fledged two-way cable system at the 1963 World Fair. Their Picturephone with Touchtone dialling (like the British View-Phone with Key-Phone dialling) was an instant hit. But nobody bought it. Some cities, including New York, actually banned it. Bell managed to install only 188 Picturephones in Chicago and 12 in Pittsburgh; though the White House, always eager for the latest electronic gadget, bought ten.

New York banned the Picturephone, and other cities did not install it, because it was grossly extravagant of bandwidth (which means that its radio waves use a lot of space) and very expensive. The Picturephone was an extraordinary, extravagant crazy leap in the dark. A total two-way video network on the same scale as the existing telephone service, or even larger, may be the ultimate objective but it cannot be the first step. Many people do not yet have an ordinary audio telephone.

Rediffusion, a British-based international company that runs television and radio stations in many countries, had a more modest ambition when they implemented their Dial-a-Program system in Dennis Port, a small resort five miles north of the Kennedys' Hyannis Port in Cape Cod, Massachusetts. Dial-a-Program uses twin-pair, not co-axial cables, but the effects are roughly similar. The station delivers 24 channels to the subscriber's set-side terminal. The subscriber presses a button to produce on the screen a list of channels, services and programmes. He can choose between most New York and Boston off-air stations (which his non-dialling neighbours cannot get), the Rediffusion local office, and several customer services like the local delicatessen, hardware store and bank.

Several other companies in America, Canada, Belgium and Japan have followed Rediffusion's lead, though with different systems. Britain's only attempt (by ITN in 1970) was squashed by the incoming Conservative Government.

The conversion of a one-way system to a two-way system is expensive but straightforward. The station needs a control desk, set-side terminals and a computer. It links the control desk to the locations (shops, banks, etc.) and installs the terminals in subscribers' homes. The station computer scans the terminals every few seconds (most computers can scan 1,000 terminals every second) to check for subscribers' requests and to link them, through the control desk, to the appropriate location.

The subscriber uses the terminal like a telephone. First, he consults Channel One which lists all the station's current channels and services. Imagine he wants to see a particular movie and then eat at a restaurant. He checks Channel One and notes that Channel Eleven has an Entertainment Guide and Channel Fifteen a Restaurant Guide. He presses button 11. He sees his favourite movie is playing at the Waldorf and decides to book two tickets. He dials a series of codes which tell the computer that subscriber 362 on Channel 11 wants to book item 45 two times in price range 3. The subscriber notices he has a choice of times: 6.30 (coded 1) and 9.00 (coded 2). He dails 2 and waits. The computer checks his credit rating and the cinema's box office and then, on the terminal panel, a green light blinks happily.

The subscriber follows roughly the same process to book a restaurant, checking on Channel Fifteen for a picture of a new vegetarian one that has opened recently.

The same computer can link him to local shops, mail order stores, offices, banks, welfare centres, travel agencies or anything else. It can also read, in reverse, the subscriber's electricity and gas meters; turn on and off his lighting and heating; preset his videotape recorder to record TV programmes as they are broadcast; and survey his property for fire and theft.

The world's largest two-way system is ATC's COMSERV in Orlando, Florida. The system links, on a one-way system, over 100,000 subscribers and so far, ATC have supplied two-way terminals to 500 of these. The wide variety of services include video consultations by a local medical doctor. In South Orange, New Jersey, subscribers can vote by cable. The station cablecasts a list of city council speakers, motions and amendments and the subscriber registers his vote by pressing one of three buttons on his set-side terminal.

Many systems, from the Leisure World Residence in Arizona to Tama New Town in Tokyo, provide complicated surveillance systems for their more elderly subscriber's homes and gardens.

HOME VIDEO PLAYERS

It sounds futuristic. Too good, or too bad, to be true. But America's most powerful corporations (CBS, AT&T, RCA, General Electric, etc) are making the dream come true. Whether you find it terrifying or most welcome – two-way cable is a fact.

Time magazine set the scene in 1970:

Cable will change the country's way of life. The copper co-axial cable, though little larger than a telephone wire, has 1,000 times the communication capacity. Washington willing, the US could be transformed into what some call the 'wired nation'. Within ten years, cable's two-way conduits could provide set-side shopping and banking, dial-a-movie, a burglar and fire watch, and facsimile print-outs of books and newspapers.

Within ten years, US cable may provide set-side bingo, electronic baby sitters, re-runs of re-runs of The Return of Peyton Place, I Love the Son of Lucy, old cartoons and *very* old movies.

The importance of cable is that its technology can cope with *both* set-side bingo and documentaries about the local housing shortage. The major TV producers and stations are keen to treat cable as a handy and profitable addition to their off-air programmes. Many vigorous and skilful video groups, however, are arguing the opposite. They want cable to provide a real extension of choice, including real 'alternative' television. They do not want ten episodes of a network hit, or even ten different network hits. They want ten truly different programmes.

Video groups in America and Canada, at least, are vigorous and skilful. Groups in Britain, the rest of Europe, Australia and Japan are less successful. Britain's current experiment with five cable stations does not include a two-way capability. The British Post Office has built two-way systems at the new towns of Washington, County Durham, and Milton Keynes and intends to build more; but the government has not yet authorized their use.

The potential of two-way cable is revolutionary. The American Cable Television Information Center summarizes its impact:

Two-way communication can convert cable systems from 'passive' to 'interactive' use, changing the nature and importance of cable services in a significant way. The change can be compared to the difference between having an AM-FM radio – a passive device – and a telephone – an interactive device which permits a communications dialogue.

At last that word 'dialogue' which originally lay at the heart of communications, but which has lately been squeezed out, returns to its proper place.

Two of the most amazing exhibits in the new communications revolution are video-discs and video-cassettes.

Both video discs and cassettes are recognizably derived from the familiar LP disc and audio-cassette. But that only makes the simple act of putting a video-disc on a turn-table, or a video-cassette into a cassette player, and producing television, even more astonishing.

It is potentially profitable too. The major American and Japanese corporations have been fighting for years over the market for both discs and cassettes. They speak persuasively of $500 worth of sales in 1975 and a billion dollars in 1980. Robert Sarnoff, Chairman of RCA, has stuck his neck out to say that in 1981 Americans will spend a billion dollars on video players and a billion dollars on discs and cassettes.

The $2-billion question, then, is what recorders? What discs? What cassettes? The tragedy (economic and artistic) is that nobody knows. The same people who argued over the right kind of colour television and the right speed for LP records are now arguing over the various kinds of video players. The crux of the argument is compatibility (in other words, does machine X play discs or cassettes made by company Y). We have seen that different countries have different standards for their television sets; the manufacturers have now compounded the problem by producing different kinds of discs and cassettes. Not one is compatible with any other.

The saga of Electronic Video Recording (EVR), a device which predates both video-discs and video-cassettes, reveals the complex and expensive wheeling and dealing that has marked the birth pangs of home video.

The saga started in the early 1960s when NASA asked CBS to develop a video recorder for the Apollo moon programme. CBS contacted Dr Peter Goldmark, their virtuoso Head of Research who had already invented colour TV and the LP record and who quickly invented EVR. The basic medium of EVR is a tiny 8·75-mm strip of film (one quarter movie-size 35 mm) which contains two tracks: one for colour and one for brightness. Cassettes hold 30 minutes' worth of film, and the pictures are played on a TV set. EVR was odd, certainly, but original. CBS used their imagination and called it 'the visual equivalent of the LP'. In 1967 (several years before even the amazing Dr Goldmark had produced a video disc or cassette) CBS formed a consortium with ICI and CIBA and started worldwide marketing plans.

The honeymoon lasted four years. Then the research

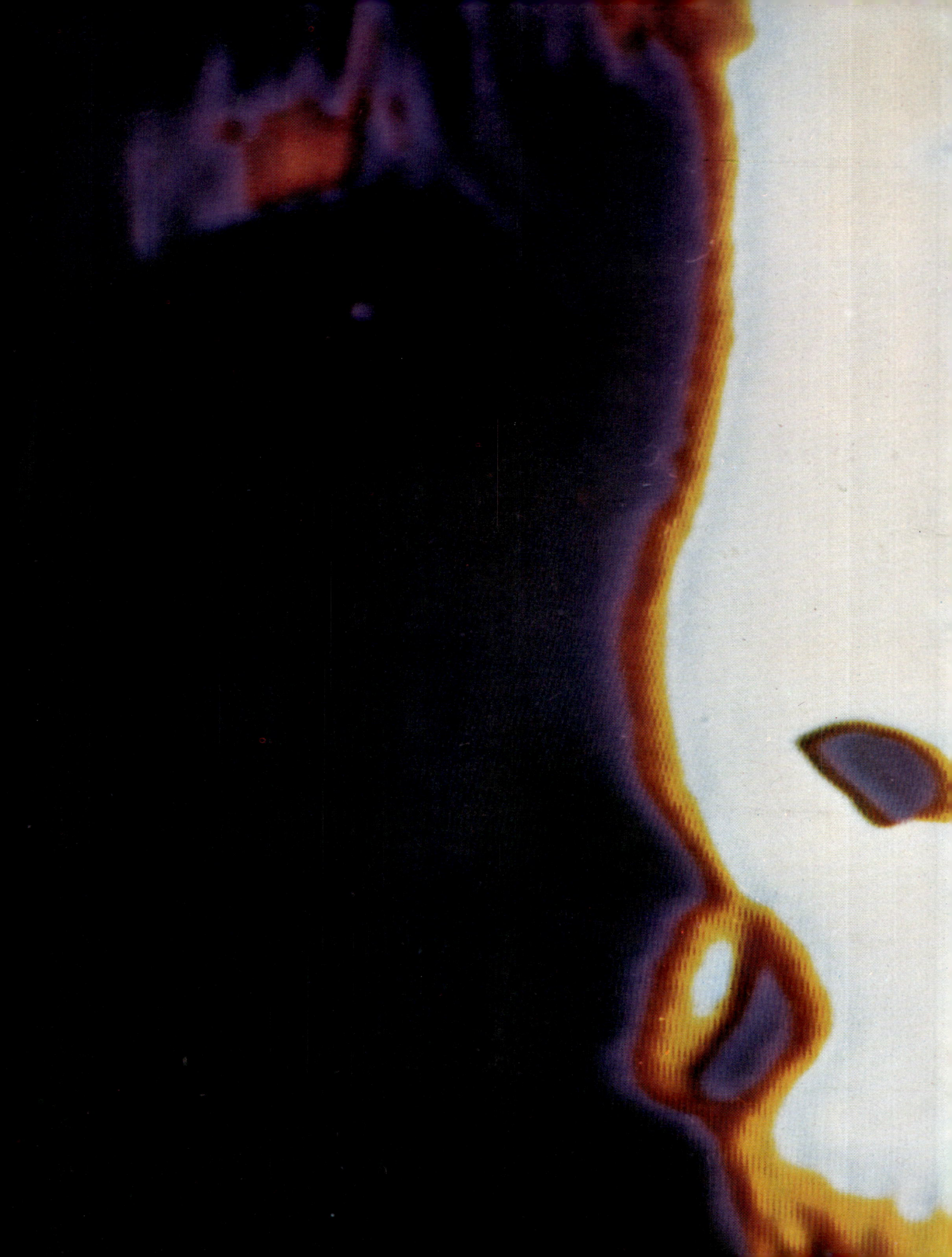

By mixing several electronic images and twisting the camera's colour controls, TV artists can produce some vivid images. . . .

bill topped £20 million and CBS quietly withdrew. ICI and CIBA (then CIBA-CEIGY) retained 51 per cent of the shares and sold the rest to four Japanese companies. After more complicated take-overs and deals (and constant rumours that EVR was dead) the six companies shared out the three main markets. In Europe, ICI and CIBA jointly own the EVR Partnership (the original Head Licensee) and run a factory in Basildon, England.

In Japan, the four Japanese companies own 66·6 per cent and ICI and CIBA 33·3 per cent of Nippon EVR and run a factory in Hiroshima. In North America, ICI, CIBA and Nippon EVR (itself part-owned by the Europeans) own EVR systems. It is a complicated story – and typically so.

Dr Goldmark, meanwhile, has left CBS and founded Goldmark Communications; and turned his attention to cable TV.

EVR is not cheap and it can play only pre-recorded material. The two factories seem to sell most of their output to hospitals (for training) and large corporations (for training and recruitment). And in several ships EVR has replaced 'another system which proved to be insufficiently rugged for use by off-duty crews'. But EVR, in spite of CBS's original extravagant claims, cannot succeed as a home video player. Most people will want either a video-disc player or a cassette machine.

The disc market, alas, is also fragmented and confused. A quick run-through will reveal the major systems. The first video-disc to be produced on a large scale was Telefunken and Decca's TeD. The TeD package consists of a player which is plugged into a TV set, and an 8-inch flimsy vinyl disc which plays for 10 minutes. The playback technique is incredible. The flimsy disc, held up by a cushion of air, whizzes round a central spindle at 1,500 rpm (compared to an LP's 33⅓ rpm). A large scoop-shaped stylus 'reads' one complete TV picture every revolution and transmits it to the TV set. Decca expect to *hire* their disc players for about half the cost of a colour TV set and *sell* the discs (a single ten-minute disc should cost around £2·50).

The other systems are completely different. RCA's SelectaVision has a 12-inch disc which revolves at 450 rpm and plays for 20 minutes; while Philips and MCA have combined to produce a player which uses a laser beam.

At the other extreme to TeD's 1,500 rpm is the Sydnor-Barent disc which revolves at a funereal 2 rpm. The 12-inch disc consists of 65,000 millimetre lens arranged in a continuous spiral.

Most manufacturers hope to produce their players and discs by the mid-1970s. The players will cost around £300, which is remarkably cheap for such a clever gadget. They do, however, have one major drawback. They can play only pre-recorded discs, and the range of discs (for some years, anyway) is likely to be restricted to mainstream movies (and pornography), hobbies, entertainment, education and travel – with the stress on the mainstream.

The real enthusiast will need a videotape cassette recorder (VCR) which, like an ordinary cassette recorder, can both record and play back. You slot the cassette into the machine, press the Forward and Record buttons and the VCR records. Then rewind, press the Forward button and the machine plays back.

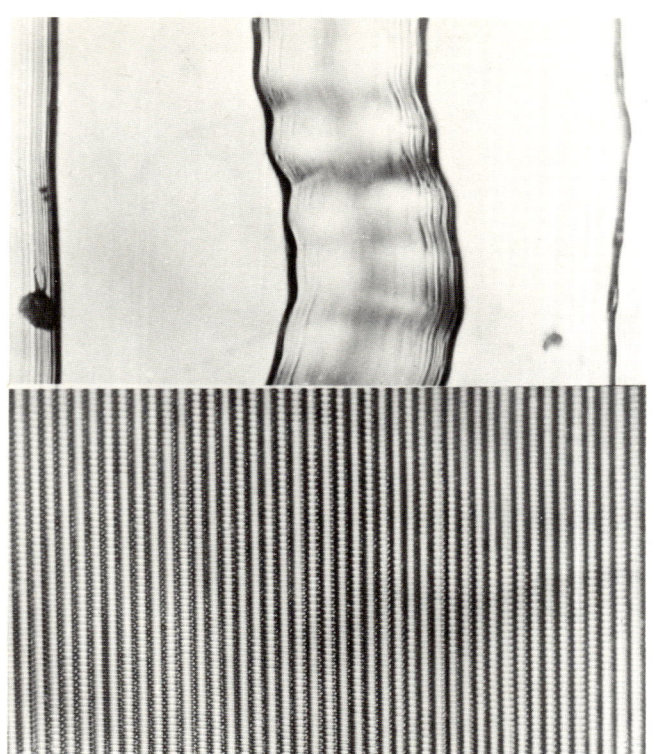

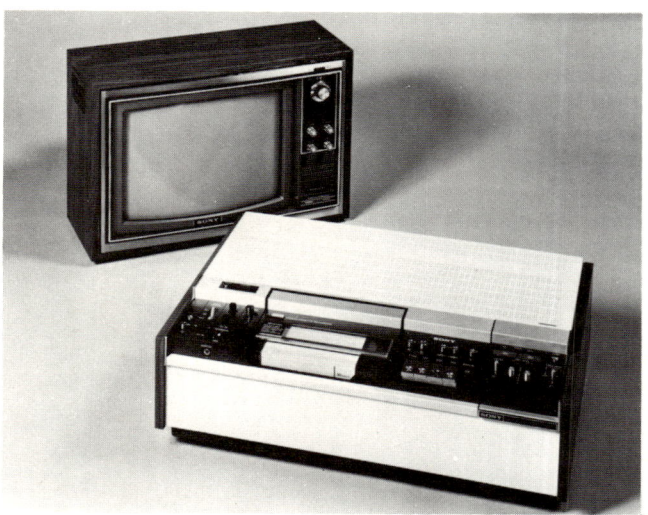

Marshall McLuhan is ecstatic about cassettes: 'They will affect every aspect of our lives, will give us new needs, goals and desires and will upset all political, educational and commercial establishments.' McLuhan does tend to exaggerate. Put more simply, cassettes give the viewer more control over his viewing. In McLuhan's terms, that is a revolution.

The basic mechanics of VCRs are similar to those of ordinary videotape machines (see Chapters 3 and 4). But each manufacturer has a different way of transferring the TV signal from the machine to the videotape; only the Japanese companies have managed to standardize their machine *and* tapes.

The first cheap VCR was the Philips VCR-1500, which was launched in 1972. The proud owner of a Philips VCR can actually be his own programme controller. He records programmes off-air (unless he owns the inferior American version which does not have this facility) or he can

120

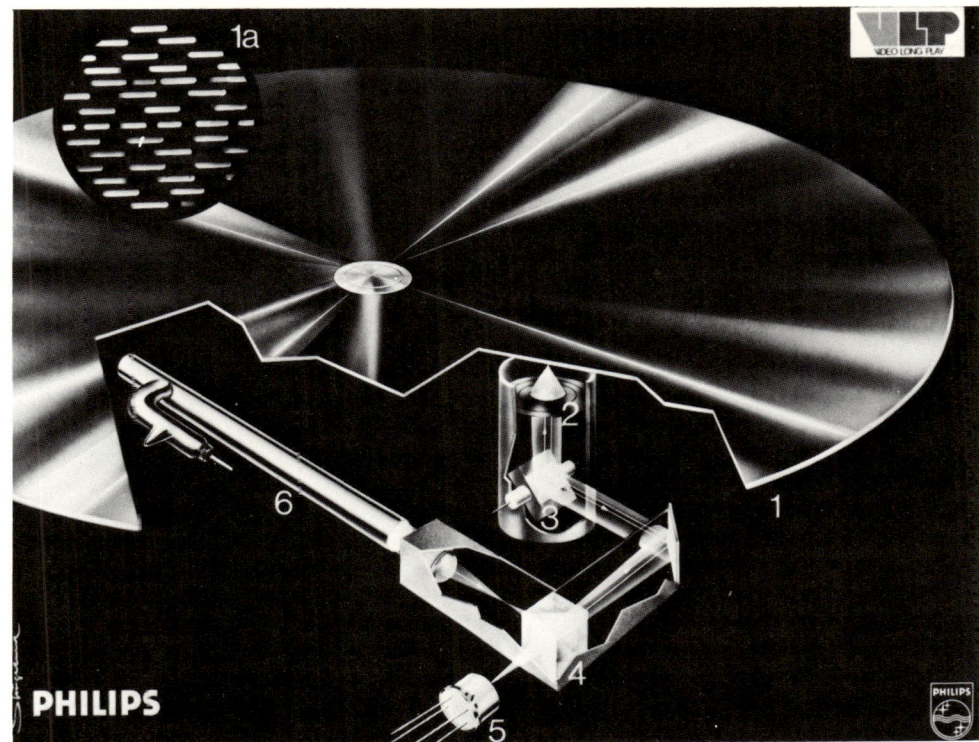

A video disc has thirteen grooves where an LP record has one; and seventeen more where the LP has none. An artist's impression shows Philip's laser disc system.

The two rivals: the Sony videotape recorder and the Philips MCA disc player. The disc unit will be much cheaper; but can play only pre-recorded material.

buy programmes from a shop or hire them from a library. He can preset the recorder to record at any time (it's as simple as presetting the oven) and he can record a programme on one channel while simultaneously watching a programme on another channel.

VCRs and cable are both devices for avoiding the pressures of peak time. For many years, peak time is likely to be reserved for top entertainment. But a cable station can transmit, and a VTR record, any programme at any time – even at 2 in the morning.

Suddenly, the official schedules become meaningless. And add a camera (Sony make a black-and-white TV camera with an 8:1 zoom lens for £200) and you have the makings of a TV studio. You can make home television which, unlike home movies, will appear on the telly.

Both video-discs and video-cassettes have this overwhelming strength: their owner can choose his programmes from a much wider range and he can control, more or less, his own programming. On condition, that is, that most discs and cassettes will fit most players.

If you make a better mousetrap, says the proverb, the world will beat a path to your door. The electronics industry seems to have made several better mousetraps, but they seem to be incompatible with the cheese.

The first years of video-discs and cassettes will be confusing and infuriating. But the problem is likely to solve itself – in the same way as everyone eventually agreed that all LP turntables should revolve at $33\frac{1}{3}$ rpm. When that happy day arrives, and you can plug your video-player into your TV set alongside your cable terminal, the Communications Revolution will have finally arrived.

Above: Teletext, a sort of TV newspaper. Right: Two of the co-axial cables which can transmit dozens of television programmes along a single wire. New technologies like ceefax and oracle, and co-axial cable, mean that television will change in many unpredictable ways in the near future.

When John Logie Baird and Philo F Farnsworth transmitted the first television pictures on their respective sides of the Atlantic they could not have conceived the results.

Both inventors, incidentally, went unrewarded. Baird, a dour Scotsman, is generally credited with 'inventing' television with his transmission of (rather shadowy) human faces in 1926. The BBC soon preferred (and rightly, too) the alternative electronic system and Baird was forgotten. He died in 1946. His American contemporary, an Idaho Mormon, demonstrated the first American television by transmitting an image of the American dollar, which revealed not only his talents but also his Mormon suspicions of what TV was really all about.

Television (images-at-a-distance) has popped up everywhere. Everyday the Earth's family of TV stations transmit their programmes to 300 million TV sets. There are a much larger number of closed-circuit television systems, from Concorde's under-the-wing cameras which monitor the aerofoils to the German systems which allow fathers, standing hygienically in an adjacent room, to gaze at their newly born babies. And community groups, increasing daily, are making their own television: local, functional and often private.

The growth of satellites and cable, especially two-way cable, is multiplying the available television channels and the opportunities for making and distributing new and different programmes

The mass production of video-discs and video-cassettes will enable people to buy, rent, lend and stock their own programmes. People have always given books for presents; soon, they will be able to give television programmes.

The hesitation over the television explosion is understandable. The Communications Revolution, or a version of it, is announced by someone, somewhere, every few months. The satellite revolution, the video revolution, the cable revolution (and the wired nation) – each has been declared to be the breakthrough that will bring sudden, total, revolutionary shifts in society.

Perhaps the reports exaggerate. The dramatic discovery of printing and gunpowder changed society only slowly. But the electronic media are different. TV's unique visual as-it-happens quality gives television an enormous power of immediacy and involvement. TV is quickly and irrevocably changing the way we behave.

Isaac Asimov has written about four revolutions: the first three were the invention of speech, writing and printing. The fourth is the invention of television which, he suggests, will come to full flower with the establishment of an international satellite system. *Time* magazine was more modest, but saying the same thing, when it claimed that 'cable will change the country's way of life'.

Nobody should repeat the classic gaffe of Britain's Astronomer Royal when, in 1955, one year before Sputnik, he declared 'Space travel is utter bilge'. But some people have come close. It is not surprising, perhaps, that the early radio broadcasters were most sceptical. Sir William Haley, then the BBC's Editor-in-Chief and later Director-General, said in 1944 that he did not like television and would not have a set in his house.

So today's hesitation over the new technologies is understandable. Few people for a start, have actually seen a satellite, a £700 portapak or a length of co-axial cable. And the idea of suspending a flimsy piece of vinyl on a cushion of air and whizzing it round at 1,500 rpm seems slightly bizarre and most unlikely to produce television. Secondly, most people tend to think of television in terms of fixed programmes and the notion that you can make your own television seems absurd. But it is already happening.

WHAT IS TV FOR?

GLOSSARY

ABC (i) ABC; a major American network. (ii) Australian Broadcasting Commission; a public-service station
AIR All India Radio; public-service station
ARD *Arbeitsgemeinschaft der öffentlichrechtlichen rundfunkanstalten der Bundesrepublik Deutschland*; Germany's senior TV network
Anik Canadian domestic satellite
BBC British Broadcasting Corporation; public-service station
CATV Community Antennae Television; one big antenna serves many TV sets
CBS Columbia Broadcasting System; a major American network
Chroma-key an electronic device for inserting one TV image into another
Comsat Communications Satellite Corporation; an American corporation which administers Intelsat
Cut an instant switch from one TV image to another used in (i) live television; (ii) recording; (iii) editing
Early Bird the first commercial satellite (1965)
Director the person in charge of a production's camera crew, etc., and responsible for its artistic aspects
EBU European Broadcasting Union; a working group of broadcasting stations
ETV Educational television
Eurovision The EBU TV network which links all its members
FCC Federal Communications Commission; the regulatory body of American telecommunications
Geo-stationary (of satellites) orbiting 23,300 miles above the Equator (in the synchronous belt) and therefore fixed, or stationary, relative to the Earth. All Intelsat satellites are geo-stationary
Ground station a receiver and/or transmitter that can receive and/or transmit TV signals, etc., to a satellite
IBA (i) Independent Broadcasting Authority; regulatory body of British ITV and independent radio. (ii) Israeli Broadcasting Authority; public-service station
Intelsat International Telecommunications Satellite; can refer to (i) the international body which has final authority over the system; (ii) the system; (iii) the satellites
ITCA Independent Television Companies Association; informal association of companies within ITV
ITN Independent Television News; ITV's news service
ITU International Telecommunications Union; UN agency which regulates world telecommunications
ITV Independent Television; British competitive commercial network of fifteen companies
Local TV a TV system operating within, and on behalf of, a particular, usually small, area
Mix a slow switch from one TV image to another. The first image fades out while the second one fades in
NBC National Broadcasting Company; a major American network (owned by RCA)
Network a TV system linking two or more TV stations in which the individual stations show their own programmes and those networked from the centre

NHK Nippon Hoso Kyokai; Japan's public-service station
NTSC National Television Standards Committee; the US colour system and the basis of PAL and Secam
Orbita Russian satellite system
ORTF Office de Radiodiffusion-Television Française; French public-service station (closed January 1, 1975)
PAL the German colour system used in Germany, Britain and countries associated with them
Portapak (originally Port-a-Pak) a portable, cheap and simple VTR with $\frac{1}{4}$-inch or $\frac{1}{2}$-inch videotape
Producer the person in charge of a production team
Public-service broadcasting a TV service, usually financed and controlled by the government, which seeks to serve its region's interests
RAI Radiotelevisone Italiana; Italian public-service station
PTV Public Television; (specifically) the informal network of American independent stations
RTC Radiotelevision Canada; Canadian public-service station (changed its name from CBC in 1974)
Secam the French colour system used in France and Russia and countries associated with them
SITE Satellite Instructional Television Experiment; Indian project
Standards the line standards (405, 525, 625 or 815 lines), colour system (NTSC, PAL or Secam) and voltage (60 or 50 hertz) of a television picture
Sync (synchronization) the maintenance of one operation in step with another. The production of a TV image depends on several electrical impulses being in *sync*
Synchronous orbit the orbit, 22,300 miles high, which makes an orbiting object stay in the same place relative to the Earth (because the Earth itself is orbiting)
Tele-generation a generation growing up in a TV society
Teleprompter an optical device which enables performers to read their scripts unobtrusively
Television the electronic reproduction, at a distance, of an image
Telstar the first satellite to provide a live link between America and Britain (1962)
TV homes the number of homes, in a given area, that have one or more TV sets
TV society a society with 90 per cent or more TV homes
Two-way cable a co-axial cable with the capacity to send signals in both directions
Video (literally) the visual part of a television signal; (figuratively) new uses of television such as 'local community video', 'video activists', etc.
Video-cassette a length of videotape enclosed in a plastic container which, when played on a VTR, winds itself on to another spool within the same container
Video-disc a flat vinyl disc (cf an LP record) which, when placed on a revolving turntable and read by a device such as a laser beam on a mechanical stylus, produces a television signal
Videotape noun: a strip of polyester coated with magnetic oxide and so able to record and playback video and audio signals. Videotape varies in width from 2 inches to $\frac{1}{4}$ inch (the wider the tape, up to 2 inches, the higher the quality of recording); verb: to record on to videotape

INDEX

AC Current 32, 33, 36
'Action replay' 36
Adrian, Max 85
Advertising 11, 88, 97 *see also* Commercials
Aerial, television 32
Aeros (German satellite) 26
Africa 12, 17, 104–5
Age of Kings, The 82
Aldrin, Edwin 19
Allen, Elizabeth 79
Allen, Jim 64
All in The Family 32, 97, 99
AM radio signal 38
American Broadcasting Corporation (ABC) 12, 21, 94ff.
 symbol 94, 95
American Gas Company 98
American's Guide to Coronation Street, The 103
American National Association of Broadcasters 21
American viewing audience 20–21
Ampex 109
An American Family 100
Andrews, Eamonn 23, 85, 90
Anik (Canadian satellite system) 26, 28
Anne, HRH Princess 86
Antenna, television 32
Ant Farm (radical video group) 111
Apollo space programme 11, 12, 18–19, 23, 117
Arab guerillas 13
Armchair Theater 64
Armstrong, Neil 11, 18
Arsenal (football team) 79
Arthur Godfrey Show, racial criticism 24
Asama Mountain Lodge, kidnapping 53
Ascent of Man, The 87
Asia 12, 17, 104–5
Asimov, Isaac 123
Assistant producer 44ff.
ATC's COMSERV (2-way cable system) 116
Atkins, Eileen 68, 69
Atlantic Ocean, satellites above 25, 26
AT&T 28, 95
Australian Broadcasting Control Board 93
Australian Broadcasting Commission (ABC) 62, 88, 92ff., 92–3
Austria, broadcasting station (ORF) 13
Autocue 32, 37
Avengers, The 64

Baglin, Bill 60
Baird, John Logie 17, 123
Baker, Richard 55
Ballistic Early Warning System (US) 26
Bangkok 24
Bangladesh, coverage of 53
Barlow at Large 83
Barron, Keith 73, 84
Barry, Michael 62, 64
Bates, Richard 65
Battle of Trafalgar 86
Beatles, The 98
Beeny, Christopher 80
Belfast, British troops in 52
Bellbird 62
Bell Telephone 116
Berger, John 86
Beverly Hillbillies, The 98
Bilko, Sgt. 96
Black September (guerilla group) 12
Blooming Youth 65
Blue Peter 86
BMEWS 1–6 (US satellite) 26
Bolt, Robert 69
Bonanza 102, 102–3, 105
Borzov, Valerie 12
Bosanquet, Reginald 55
Bowen, John 64
Brambell, Wilfrid 82
Brazil 102–3,
 use of satellite 26
Bristol, cablecasting at 112;
 channel 110
British Broadcasting Corporation (BBC) 12, 13, 16, 17, 23, 25, 56, 78, 102
 coverage of Middle East war 56ff.
 radio 88
British Petroleum 103
British Relay Cable Company 112

Bronowski, Dr. Jacob 87
Brown, Margaret 81
Burch, Dean 112
Burnett, Hugh 80
Burstall, Christopher 81

Cablecasting, in Britain 112
 in Netherlands 113
Cable companies 112
Cable television 107ff., 111ff.
Cable, two-way 116
Cairo 60, 61
Campbell, Patrick 68
Camera, Apollo 16, 18–19
 Australia 36
 Britain 36
 -card 33
 CBS colour 17
 EMI 200 colour 32
 film 32
 image-orthicon 33
 lens 37
 men 44, 56
 Portapak 107ff.
 Pye mark VI 32
 scanning 33, 36
 studios, in 44ff.
 television 32, 33ff., 38, 39
 vidicon 33, 56
Canada
 Anik satellite system 26
 broadcasting corporation (RTC) 68
 Canadian Broadcasting Corporation (CBC) 88
Cannon 97, 102
Cape Canaveral 26
Carson, Johnny 98
Case, Martin 73
Cathode tube, in television set 38
Cathy Come Home 62, 85
CATV (Community Antenna Television – cable television) 112
Ceefax 122
Chamberlain, Neville 78
Chataway, Christopher 81
Chayevsky, Paddy 62
Chicago University, television survey 23
China 17, 25, 28, 77, 88
Chroma-key, in production 36, 38
CIBA 117, 120
CIBA-CEIGY 120
Civilisation 84
Clark, Kenneth 84
Clarke, Arthur C. 25, 29
Climpson, Roger 53
Close-up (CU) 33, 45
Co-axial cable 116ff., 122
Collings, David 85
Collins, Pauline 69
Colour disc 17
Colour standard 32
Colour systems 104–5
Columbia Broadcasting System (CBS) 21, 53, 54, 56, 95, 96, 97, 111, 117
 colour camera (1947) 17
 symbol 94–5
Columbo 32
Columbus, Christopher 11
Comsat, booking agency for Intelsat 25, 28
Commercials 90, 95
 see also Advertising
Communications Technology Satellite (CTS) 29
Community Access Video 107, 110
Comte, Arthur 105
Control rooms 40, 44
Cope, Kenneth 83
Corbett, Harry H. 82
Coronation, Elizabeth II 23
 George VI 23, 23
Coronation Street 102, 102, 103, 103, 105
Cosmos (Russian satellite) 26
Country Matters 65
Courier satellite 26
Cricket, action replays 36
Crockett, Davy 96
Cronkite, Walter 21, 55, 56
Culloden 87
Curran, Sir Charles 100
'Cuts', in production 36, 37ff., 44, 49
Czechoslovakia, Russian invasion of 13

Damascus 60, 61
Day, Doris 94
Decca TeD (video disc) 120
Delius 85
Delta, rocket 26
Derby (races) 79
Desmonde, Jerry 79
Dial M for Murder 62
Dimbleby, Richard 81
Director 36ff., 44ff.
Documentaries 21
Documentary, dramatised 62, 80, 87
Dougall, Robert 23, 54, 55
Drama, on television 44, 62ff.
Dr. Who 64
'Dry runs' 45
Dubbing 44

Early Bird satellite 26
Earth stations 25
East Germany, exclusion from Comsat 28
Editing 44
 Upstairs Downstairs 75
Educational television 104
Egypt and Middle East War 56, 60ff.
Eisenhower, Dwight D. 26
El Al (air lines) 56–7
Electronics 12, 32ff., 36, 38, 56
Electronic Video Recording (EVR) 117f., 120
Elizabeth II, coronation of 23
Elizabeth R 65
EMI 200 colour camera 32
European Broadcasting Union (EBU) 12
Eurovision 12
Evening News, CBS 56
Ewing, Barbara 65
Explorer, satellite 28

Face to Face 80
Family at War, A 102
Farnsworth, Philo F. 123
Faulds, Chris 57
Federal Communications Commission (FCC) 95, 99, 111, 112
Ferguson, Don (Visnews) 53
Fielding, John 57
Film, crew 61
 director 44
 dubbing 44
 editing 44
 high speed Ektachrome 56
Finch, John 65
First outside broadcast 23, 23
Floor manager 44, 49
Fonteyn, Margot 80
Football 79
Forsyte Saga, The 62
France, broadcasting organisation (ORTF) 105
Frank, Reuven 52
Freeman, John 80, 81
Frost, David 83

Gallery *see* Control room
Gandhi, Mrs. Indira 29
Gardiner, Andrew 55
Garnett, Tony 64, 65
General Strike (1921) 88
Geneva Convention 61
Geneva, Intelsat booking agency 25
Germany 17, 21, 78, 102, 102, 103, 103
 broadcasting consortium (DOZ) 12
 broadcasting organisation (ARD) 56, 88, 103
 electronic trickery 36ff., 38
 Symphonie (satellite) 28
George VI, coronation 23
Gibraltar, solitary channel 77
Gioia, Signor 113
Glenn, Col. John 98
'Global village' 11, 12
Golan Front 60, 61
Gold disc, in replays 36
Goldmark, Dr. Peter 117
Golym (computer) 12
Grade, Sir Lew 90, 94, 103
Graduate, The 95
Graef, Roger 86
Granger, Derek 65
Graves, Keith 60
Greece 25, 88
Green, Hughie 90
Green, John 45
Greene, Hugh 54
Greene, Lorne 102, 102–3
Grove Family, The 80
Guerilla television 107
Gurney, Rachel 69

Hackett, Buddy 98
Haley, Sir William 123
Hamlet, studio production 62
Harding, Gilbert 79
Hard Labour 62
Harris, Larry 60
Harwood, John 57
Hawaii Five-O 97
Hawkesworth, John 68, 69, 75
Helen, A Woman of Today 65, 65
Henry VIII, The Six Wives of 65
Here's Lucy 102
Hodson, Christopher 72, 74
Hole, Tahu 54
Hollywood, television films from 64
Homicide 92–3
Hopkins, John 64
Horne, Jim 87
Houston 19
Huntley-Brinkley Report 56

ICI 117, 120
Independent Broadcasting Authority (IBA) 12, 54
Independent Television (ITV) 54, 88, 90–91
 Associated Television (ATV) 90, 94
 Granada Television 12, 90, 103
 London Weekend Television (LWT) 68, 69, 74, 90, 103
 Thames Television 90–91
Independent Television News (ITN) 54, 55, 55, 56ff., 57
India 17, 77
 broadcasting organisation (AIR) 29
 satellites 26, 29
Intelsat (International Telecommunication System) 25, 26, 28ff., 61
International Telecommunication Union (ITU) 26, 111
Intersputnik (Russian satellite) 28
Inventors, The 92
Israel, broadcasting organisation (IBA) 104
 Middle East War 56ff.
 Olympic team 12, 13
 policy in Intelsat 28
Italy 13
 broadcasting organisation (RAI) 12, 61, 88, 113
It's A Knockout! 84

Japan 12, 20, 24, 88, 102–3, 104
 broadcasting organisation (NHK) 52, 53, 56, 88, 92, 103
Johnson, Lyndon 23, 54
 use of teleprompter 37
Johnson, Nicholas 95, 112
Jones, Elwyn 64

Kee, Robert 81
Kendall, Kenneth 53
Kennedy, Caroline 23
Kennedy, Jackie 52
Kennedy, John, assassination 21ff.
 policy over Intelsat 28
Kennedy, Robert 23
Kennedy Martin, Troy 64
King Heroin 113
Kinnear, Roy 83
KNET (Los Angeles) 100
Kraft Theatre play 94–5

Lamb, Kenneth 81
Lancashire, Chief Constable, complaint of *Z Cars* 83
Lancaster, Burt 103
Laski, Margharita 79
Law-Giver, The 103
Lawrence of Arabia 94
Lenin 85
Licence, television 88
Lighting 44
Lindley, Richard 60
Line standard 32
Little Farm, The 65
Lloyd, David 44
Local Origination (cable television) 112
Local television 106ff.
Location filming 44
 for *Upstairs Downstairs* 72
Lone Ranger, The 94–5
Long, Marceau 105
Long Day's Journey Into Night 65
Lunik (USSR satellite) 25

Mahoney, John 56
Malraux, Andre 85
Malta, broadcasting station (MTS) 102
Marsh, Jean 68, 68

125

Marshall, Bryan 65
'Mass Media' concept 23—4
Matlock Police 92—3
MCA 120
McCarthy, Joseph 94—5
McClelland, Douglas 93
McCord, James 100
McGrath, John 65
McLuhan, Marshall 11, 77, 120
McTaggart, James 64
Medium Close-up (MCU) 45
Mercer, David 64
Michelmore, Cliff 83
Microphones, overhead 49
Middle East Media (news agency) 61
Middle East War 56—61
Miller, Joan 78
Mills, Annette 80
Mill Village, Canada 25
Minow, Newton 99
Mitchell, Warren 85
Mixes, in production 36, 37ff.
  in variety 37—8
Molyna satellites 26—8
Monitor 11, 12, 44
Monty Python 86
Moon, communication with men on 25
  landing on 11, 12, *18*
Moorfoot, Rex *81*
Mormon 123
Morse 29
Muffin The Mule 80
Muggeridge, Malcolm 83
Murray-Brown, Jeremy *81*
Murrow, Ed 53

Nagra recorder 56
NASA 11, 28—9, 117
National Broadcasting Corporation (NBC) 17, 21, 52, 94—5, 96
Nationalised television companies 105
National Viewers and Listeners Association (NVALA) 24, 86
Netherlands Broadcasting Foundation 104
Newman, Stanley 64
News 12, 21
  bulletin 52
  coverage 52ff.
  editor 56ff.
  organisation over Middle East War 56ff.
  readers 37, *39*, 53
  teleprompter, use of by 37
  studio 53
'New Television' 107, 113
'New World' 11
New York City 11, 17, 24, 107
New Zealand, broadcasting organisation (NZBC) 105
Nicholson, Michael 57
Nicol, Bill 60
Nielsen ratings 20
Nigeria 53, 77
Night Out, A 64
Nixon, Richard 95, 96
North Korea, exclusion from Comsat 28
No Trains To Lime Street 65
NTSC (colour standard) 32, 103

Olivier, Sir Laurence 65
Olympic Games, 21st. 12, *13*
Open Door 87
Oracle Receiver 122
Orbita (Russian satellite system) 26
O'Rourke, Terence 45
Osborne, Andrew 64
Oscar (satellite) 29
Oswald, Lee Harvey 23, *23*, 52

Pacific Ocean, satellite above 25
PAL (colour standard) 32, 103
Palestine, guerilla group 12
Pallisers, The 64
Panorama 80, *81*
Panther Valley Television Company 112
Parker, Fess 96
PA System 44
Paul Hogan Show 92—3
Paul, Jeremy 69, 72
Percival, Lance 83
Perfect Stranger, A (episode of *Upstairs Downstairs*), production of 72—75

Peyton Place 64, 105
Philip's laser-disc system *120*
Philip's MCA disc player *120*
Philip's VCR-1500 120
Phillip, David 57
Phosphur dots 37, *39*
Picture Page 78
Picture phone 116
Pioneer (unsuccessful US moon satellite) 26
Pinter, Harold 64
Plesetsk (rocket pad) 26
Play School 82
Please Sir! 103
Poland 102—3
Polaroid pictures 11
Pope, The 25
Popelka, Dubos *13*
Portapak 107, *108*, 109ff.
  Sony portapak *110*
Port, Leo 92—3
Poseidon Adventure, The 94
Potter, Dennis 64, *84*
Poulson, John 90
Press, the 21
Production 32ff.
  team 44, 45, 64
Programme market, international 102
Programme presenter 45
Public Television (PTV), US 100
Pye Mark VI camera *32*

Quello, James 95
Quizzes 21

Radical Software (magazine) 107
Radio, source of news 11, 12, 21, 23
Raindance (radical video group) 111
RCA 95, 96, 117
  Selecta Vision 120
Reception 32, 38, *39*
Recorder, Nagra 56
Red Cross, The 61
Rediffusion Cable Company 112
Rediffusion Dial-a-Program 116
Rediffusion 23
Rees, Norman 60
Rehearsals 45
  of *Upstairs Downstairs* 73
Reith, Lord 88, 93
Religion 21
Reporters 61
  freelance 44
  Middle East War 56, *60*
Researchers 44
Reynolds, Burt *98*
Rickles, Don *98*
Rocket, Delta *26*
Rocket pads 26
Ruby, Jack 23, *23*
Rushton, William 83
Russell, Bertrand 80
Russell, Ken *85*
Russia 13, *13*, 25, 26, 28, 77, 88

Saccho, Beppo 113
Sagitta (production company) 68
Sam 65, 90
Samos-91 (US satellite) 26
Sanford and Son 97, 99
Sandford, Jeremy 64
Sarnoff, Richard 117
Satellites, Aeros 26
  artificial 25
  ATS-6 29
  'broadcast' 26·
  communication technology (CTS) 29
  Cosmos 538—542 26
  Courier 26
  'distribution' 26
  'domestic' 26
  early TV programme by 26
  earth stations 26, 60
  Explorer, US 28
  first 25
  Instructional Television Experiment (SITE) 29
  Intelsat 25ff.
  link with Asia/America 53
  Molyna, USSR 28
  Oscar 29
  Orbita, USSR 28
  over oceans 12

Symphonie, France-Germany 28
  system, Canada 28
  television companies and 26
  Telstar, US 28
  use of 26
Satire show 83
Scanning, by camera 33, 36
Schenectady 62
Scott, Gary 19
Script, editor 64
  teleprompter 37
  writers 64
Secam (colour standard) 32
Second World War 16
Sekigun, Rengo 53
Selling of programmes see Programme market
Sesame Street 100, *100*
Seven Little Australians 92—3
Seymour, Gerald 57
Shah of Persia 25
Shaughnessy, Alfred 68, 69
Sheffield, cablecasting at 112
Shulman, Milton 79
Silvers, Phil *96*
Simeoni, Sara *13*
Sinai, battle on 60, 61
Singleton, Valerie *86*
Singley, Ed *94*
Six Wives of Henry VIII, The 65
Sloan Report (1971) 112
Small, William 54
Smith, Anthony 81
Soccer, action replay 36
Society of Film and Television Arts (SFTA), annual awards 23, 68, 69
Softly, Softly 105
  Doldini, John 57
Sony Portapak *110*
Sony Videotape recorder *120*
Sound recordist 44, *49*
Southern Segregationalists 24
Southgate, Robert 60
Space Between Words, The 86
Spain 11, 12, 25, 57, 88
Speight, Johny 85
Spitz, Mark 12
Sport 21, *32*
Sputnik 25, 123
Standard, colour 32
Standard, line 32
Serling, Rod 62
Steptoe and Son 82, 99
Studio 32, 40, 44ff., *44*
Studio discussion, examination of 45, *49*
Studio director 44, 45
Studio production, of *Hamlet* 62
Suez Canal 61
Sullivan, Ed *98*
Summers, Tony 60
Sunday Rap 44
Supermarket Sweep 98
Surveillance system 116
Swindon, cablecasting at 112
Sydnor-Barent disc 120
Syrian Arab Television SAT 60

Tape, use of in production 32
Tarlton, Robert J. 112
Technicians 17
TelApart (cable television service) 106
Tel Aviv 56, 60, 61
Tele Biella 113
Tele-cine 36
  machine 45
Telecommunications 25
Telecommunication Journal 26
Telefunken (video disc) 120
Telephone 11, 28
Teleprompter 37ff., *32*
Telesat (Canadian equivalent of Comsat) 28
Teletext 122
Television Act (Australia) 93
Television, aerial *32*
  agency 68
  antenna 32
  broadcasters 12
  club 12
  bill to ban programmes 24
  definition of 32
  effect on society 23—4
  future of 104ff.

  guide US 68
  'homes' 20
  inventor of first broadcast 17
  Programme Standards (book) 93
  receiving apparatus 17
  signals 12, 32, 36
  sets, homes with 17, *20*
  'Society' 17
  source of news 21
  studio *32*
  transmissions, first regular 16
Telex transmission, Comsat bias towards 28
Telstar (1962) 26, 28
Thailand 24, 102—3
That Was The Week That Was 83
The 64,000 Dollar Question 96
Thermopylae, bridge of 25
This Day Tonight 92—3
This Is Your Life 90
This Week 57
Till Death Us Do Part 32, *85*, 99, 102—3
Time-Life 103
Tokyo 24
Tonight 83
Top Value Television (TVTV) 111
Trade Unions 21
Transmission of television signal 32ff., 38, 45, 61
Trevor, William 64
Trickery in production 36ff.
Two-way cable 116, 117

Ugandan broadcasting station (UTS) 102
Ulster, coverage of 53
UNESCO 104
United Nations, members joining Intelsat 25
United Nations and SITE 20
Unscripted play 62
UPI 21, 23, 61
Upstairs Downstairs 33, 68, 70, *71*, 68ff., *72*, 75, 80

van Doren, Charles *96*
Vatican city 12
Video-cassette 117
Video Cassette Recorder (VCR) 120, 121
  see also Philip's VCR-1500 120
Video-disc 117, 120, *120*
Video-player 117
Videotape (VT) 37, 44, 45, 49, 56, 75, 109, 110
  recorders (VTR) 45, 107, *108*, 109
Vietnam 52—54
Viewers, early 17
Viewing pattern 20
View-phone 116
VHF 111
Violence, protest at *84*
Vivat Vivat Regina 69
Vote Vote Vote for Nigel Barton 64

War and Peace 65
Wargame 84
Watch With Mother 82
Ways of Seeing 86
Wednesday Play 64, *85*
Weekend World 57
Weldon, Fay 69, 72
Wellingborough, cablecasting at 112
Westerns 11
Western Electric, proposal to distribute films to cinema by satellite 29
Wharf Road Mob, The 80
What's My Line? 79, 100
White House 23, 28
Whitehouse, Mary 86
Who's Who? 21
Willings, Peter 45
Wireless World (magazine) 25
Wise, Herbert 64
World At War 90
World's Fair (1963) 116
World In Action 90
Worldwide television, chart 104—5
Writers' Guild, The 69
Wyatt, Woodrow *81*

Yugoslavia, broadcasting organisation (JRT) 12

Z Cars 64, 83

ACKNOWLEDGMENTS

The publishers would like to thank the following individuals and organizations for their kind permission to reproduce the photographs in this book:

ABC (Australia): 92 left, 94 left; ABC News (US): 55 below right; ARD (Germany): 102 below right; ATV (UK): 64 above left; Austarama Television Ltd: 93 below right; Australian Television: Channel 7–53 above left, 92 right, Channel 9–93 top left, 93 below, Channel 10–93 above right; Autocue Ltd: 32 below; Barnaby's Picture Library: 82 centre; BBC (UK): 16, 17 below, 32–33 above, 33 below, 36, 44, 52 above, 52–53 below, 55 left, 62–63, 64–65, 66–67, 78 above left, 78 centre, 78 below right, 79 centre, 79 below right, 80–81, 82 above, 82 below, 82–83 centre, 83, 84 above, 84 centre, 84 right, 85, 86 left, 87 above, 87 below left, 88, 96 below right, 100 below left, 102 left, 103; Bishop's Television News Service: 90 centre right; Camera Press Ltd: 53 below right; CBS (US): 17 above, 53 above right, 55 centre right, 96 below left, 98 right, 99 below left; Children's Television Workshop: 101 right; Decca Radio and Television: 120 above; Mark Edwards: 40–43; Ghana Radio and Television Times: 76 centre; GPO London: 122 below; Granada Television (UK): 65 right, 90 above, 90 bottom left, 102 centre right; Greek Television Guide: 77 below; John Hillelson Agency Ltd (Bruno Barbey): 4–5; IBA (UK): 122 above; Bernie Ilson: 99 above right; Inter-Action: 108 left, 108 centre right, 108–109 above; ITN (UK): 50–51, 54–55 below, 57–60; Komuczixi: 13 below; Liberation Films: 107; London Weekend Television (UK): 33 below, 39, 64 below left, 68 right, 69–75, 90 centre left; Charles Maplestone: 86 right; National Aeronautics and Space Administration: 10–11, 18–19; NBC (US): 55 above centre, 94 centre, 94 right, 99 centre right, 99 bottom right, 102 above right; Nigerian Broadcasting Radio and TV Times: 76 above left; Octopus Books Ltd: 87 below right; David Paradine Productions: 23 right; Philips Electrical Ltd: 121; Pictorial Press Ltd: 24 below right; Dick Polak: 2–3, 30–31, 34–35, 45–49, 127; Popperfoto: 24 above; Radio Times Hulton Picture Library: 23 left, 76 below left, 79 below left; Radio TV Corriere: 77 above; Rediffusion (UK): 106, 108 below right, 110 right; The Science Museum, London: 16 inset; Sony (UK) Ltd: 110 above left; Spectrum Colour Library: 1, endpapers; Keith Stone: 12, 79 above left; Sundial Publications Ltd: 84 below; Syndication International: 12–13, 13–14, 22; Tasmania TV Times: 77 centre; Teleprompter: 113; Thames Television (UK): 90 below left, 90 bottom right, 91; *TV for Everybody*: 78 above right, 89; *TV Guide* (US): 68 left, 76 below right, 95, 96 above, 97, 98 left, 99 above left, 100 above left, 100–101; TV Teleguia, Cablevision, SA: 76 above right; Anno Waldorf: 38, 118–119; Yorkshire Television (UK): 90 centre below